Modelling
IN COLD PORCELAIN

TOMBI PECK
& ALAN DUNN

PUBLISHING

First published 1998 by B. Dutton Publishing Limited

Alfred House, Hones Business Park, Farnham,
Surrey GU9 8BB

ISBN 0 9532588 07

Publisher: Beverley Dutton
Editor: Jackie Tetley
Design: Barby Lock
Photography by Alister Thorpe

Printed in England by MPG Colour Limited,
Northamptonshire

*C*old porcelain is an exciting new medium which has arrived in Britain from the Southern Hemisphere.

Cold porcelain is a misnomer! There is actually no porcelain in most of the manufactured paste and in none of the home-made paste that we know of. The name comes from the translation of 'Porcelaina Fria' which is the Argentinian for cold porcelain. In Mexico it is called 'Porcelanicron' and in Brazil 'Biscuit Paste'.

I first heard about it when my friend Muffie MacKenzie said she'd been introduced to a new craft medium when she was visiting South Africa. After a certain amount of begging, she kindly gave me the recipe she had been given by a mutual friend, Eleanor Rielander. Eleanor in turn had been given the recipe when at an ICES Convention in America.

As we couldn't get the glue mentioned in the recipe, Alan and I started experimenting with every glue we could lay our hands on. One worked particularly well, but we found it had been discontinued. We tried persuading the manufacturer to continue with the product but they wanted us to order six tons of it - impossible!

A visit to another ICES Convention by Alan, Cynthia Venn and David and Margaret Ford really got us moving. Alan brought back a recipe in a Spanish language magazine published by Titi and Oscar Pena. Getting all the ingredients was very difficult (Japanese rice flour and other oddities). It was also made with Elmer's glue, and of course that was not obtainable here at that time. Cynthia Venn then gave us a simplified recipe given to her in Florida. More experimentation by Alan and myself and we finally cracked it, each finding a glue which made a good paste with very different properties which enabled us to develop the art.

We added oil paints, we added acrylics, we added gouache, we added food colouring! Many paste food colours tend to fade. Squires Kitchen colours are colour fast in most recipes. The paint which affects the consistency of cold porcelain least appears to be gouache.

Some people working in cold porcelain like painting their pieces with diluted oil paints. Alan and I by and large still prefer to dust powder colours onto our pieces. As some of the sugarcraft dusts fade we persuaded a manufacturer to produce a range of craft dusts. These are colour fast and the range is very bold. We now use a mixture of sugarcraft colours, craft dust colours and occasionally diluted oil paints and gouache to decorate our pieces.

The applications that cold porcelain can be used for are growing by the day as we all experiment. It is a very exciting, vibrant new craft with a wonderful future. Alan and I feel most privileged to be able to present to you some of our discoveries.

The thing one needs to work hard to overcome is the shrinkage factor. All the cold porcelain pastes, whether home-made or manufactured, have a tendency to shrink. This takes a great deal of getting used to. The process can be very amusing, but is sometimes extremely frustrating!

Most of the projects in this book can also be made in sugar. The only piece I would not recommend people try to copy is the head. It is possible to create it out of sugar, but not using the same methods outlined in this book. All the flowers, leaves and arrangements can be copied in sugar, omitting the use of glue (except for joining together the stamens) and using egg white instead to stick flowers and leaves to the wires.* All pieces created in sugar would turn out about twenty percent larger than those made in cold porcelain.

*For health and hygiene reasons B. Dutton Publishing Ltd. does not recommend the use of raw egg white as a sticking agent. Suggested alternatives are gum arabic or sugar glue.

Contents

Working with Cold Porcelain

*A*lthough it may seem a daunting task at first, working with cold porcelain is a rewarding experience. Once basic techniques have been learnt, almost anything can be attempted! This section introduces some of the skills required when using cold porcelain in general, as well as focusing particularly on methods for making flowers and leaves. Although these are, on the whole, similar to techniques used in sugarcraft, there are some important differences.

A list of the main equipment that has been used throughout the book can be found on page 62.

Handling Cold Porcelain

Whilst there are similarities between sugarcraft and cold porcelain techniques, there are some basic rules that need to followed if success is to be achieved with ease.

Home-made Paste

To begin with, it is important that the paste is well-kneaded: this will ensure that it is the right consistency to work with. If the paste is slightly tacky, then try using a tiny amount of cold cream on your fingers whilst kneading it, being very careful not to add too much as this can have an adverse effect - toughening the paste and making it very difficult to use. If this does happen we suggest that you add a few drops of warm water to the paste, which will sometimes (depending upon how tough the paste is)

bring it back to a reasonable working consistency, however once home-made paste has toughened it is usually wiser to use it for rose knobs and so on!

It is important to grease the work-board with a small amount of cold cream, removing most of it with kitchen paper, before rolling out the cold porcelain. This will prevent the paste from sticking to the board (again be very careful not to use too much as this can also contribute to the paste toughening). Use cornflour on the surface of the paste if it feels tacky, especially when using veiners and fine cutters.

Asi-es Paste

This paste, being developed in Argentina, prefers to be handled in warm conditions. It is important to knead the paste well, avoiding the use of cold cream in the initial stages, and to work in a warm room, avoiding direct draughts. The paste, if you prefer, can be warmed gently, while still in its packet, on top of a radiator. If this paste toughens then it can be brought back to life again with the addition of warm water; the results are much more successful than with a home-made paste, as long as you have not added too much paint! This paste prefers to be handled un-coloured, although it will co-operate to a certain extent if colour is added.

Glue and Water

When making large or intricate flowers where extra hold is needed, Hi-tack craft glue should be used undiluted. However in the case of attaching fine petals (for example on a rose), it is better to dilute the glue with a small amount of water. This diluted glue can be painted onto the petal or piped through a monojet glue dispenser. Water can also be used to stick petals together and for moistening wires that are to be used for individually wired petals and leaves. We have also developed an alternate method of moistening wires, now used gleefully by most of our students, which is commonly known as 'lick 'n' stick', but this is not compulsory!

Colouring Cold Porcelain

The finish of dried cold porcelain is smooth and can be rather plastic-looking. This effect is somewhat diminished by the addition of Permanent White gouache. The more white gouache you add to the paste the less translucent the petals or leaves become. Colour added to paste makes working the cold porcelain more difficult and it darkens quite dramatically as the paste dries and shrinks. When the petals and leaves are partially or fully dry they can be further coloured by painting with water colours, acrylics, or oils used with a little thinners and/or dusted with permanent food colours or craft dusts.

The delicate use of colour is particularly important when making leaves. Colour the paste very lightly with Sap Green gouache. The veins of most plants seem to be paler than the rest of the leaf; if you now deepen the colour on the surface of the leaves it is very easy to leave the veins pale. If they are darker than the leaf, or are a different colour it is easier to paint these colours into these exposed veins. The underside of leaves tend to be paler than the upper surface. A combination of painting and dusting works well.

It is better to dust leaves and petals when they are 'leather hard', (firm, but not quite dry). The dusts tends to stick more easily at this stage.

If the dust goes on patchily it is very likely that you have used too much cream. This can be prevented by gently washing the petals and leaves, wiping them with an art wipe or baby wipe (without lanolin) or brushing over them with a little thinner. Another reason dust adheres patchily is poor quality brushes or brushes of the wrong shape. The surface of dried cold porcelain damages sable brushes very quickly. High quality artificial fibre brushes are preferable. A good range to buy are those by Robert Simmons. The angled shaders are particularly useful. Do not use round brushes for dusting. They should be used for adding fine detail only.

When painting with oils you should use oil paintbrushes. It is very useful to add a few drops of liquid drier to your thinners. This will speed up the drying of the oil paints. We use 'Blackfriar Terrebine Liquid Drier' which can be ordered from smaller DIY shops. When painting with oils apply a minute amount of thinners to the petals or leaves before adding any paint. Use very little paint, and you should use more of a scrubbing action rather than brushing evenly. Once you have put on your tiny amount of paint and thinners, spread it using a dry brush (keep wiping your brushes on kitchen paper) and then remove the excess with a third dry brush. At this stage you can dust over the oils, or you can leave the leaf or petal to dry now if you prefer.

When dusting it is sensible to use a different brush for each colour. This prevents your work from developing a 'muddy' look. If the colour is darker than you want lighten it with Squires Kitchen Edelweiss sugarcraft dust. This white does not give patchy white streaks.

If petals and leaves have dried completely before dusting it is best to moisten them slightly first. This can be done with a damp piece of jaycloth or a baby wipe.

Do not try to dust over something which is too moist. The moisture then becomes counterproductive. Your brush will become clogged as more and more moisture is picked up by the bristles; the dust will cling to the bristles rather than to the surface of the petal or leaf.

Glazing Petals and Leaves

Glazing cold porcelain serves several purposes.

1. It protects the surface of your piece against damage from moisture (in most cases you can dust cold porcelain pieces with a slightly damp cloth, but only if the surface has been sealed or just painted with oil paints).

2. It gives flowers and leaves a more natural look.

3. If you dust your leaves and flowers glazing is required to 'set' the dust so it does not rub off.

Most petals are matt or have a slight gleam. In cold porcelain this sheen can make the finished product look like plastic.

Petals look best sealed with a matt spray. Humbrol make a matt spray but it is packaged in very small cans. Plasti-kote produce sprays in matt, satin and gloss. The matt can be difficult to track down as very

few DIY shops seem to stock this. It can be purchased from floristry sundriesmen.

Great care must be taken when spraying flowers and leaves. Your first concern once again is that of health and safety. These sprays are extremely inflammable and you should avoid inhaling them. It is once again important to wear a mask and to work in a well-ventilated area preferably without drafts.

Be careful to spray petals only once. Two applications of a matt spray can add a slight sheen. A piece can very easily be ruined by too much glazing.

Glazing leaves does not present as great a problem. There are many products on the market which are very suitable for glazing leaves. An aerosol spray on leaves is quick but with a varnish which can be diluted with water, a greater differentiation of sheens can be achieved. You can, if you prefer, use confectioners' glaze on cold porcelain leaves as well. This does not, however, give the leaves treated this way any protection against moisture (they could not be dusted with a damp cloth). In the beginning it does mean that you can achieve the finish you want because you are using a product with which you may already be familiar.

A good varnish for use on leaves is Anita's 'Water Clean-up Polyurethane Découpage Varnish'. It comes in gloss, semi-gloss and satin. They are milky looking liquids which dry clear.

The gloss produces a very high gloss which is suitable for some berries and leaves. The semi-gloss and satin diluted with water give very good results. The initial purchase price seems expensive but as they are used diluted in most cases they last very well. The leaves are better dipped into the varnish as opposed to painting on the varnish which can move the dust. The coating of cream left on the grooved board after cleaning will leave a film on the underside of the leaf. This will prevent the glaze from being as glossy on the underside of the leaf as on the top, which is more natural.

When glazing, be careful to protect the surfaces on which you are working. A plastic tablecloth works well. Plastic ice-cream containers are suitable for using as dipping trays. Place dipped leaves on baking parchment to dry. Leaves and petals painted with oil paints must be completely dry before glazing or the varnish may become mottled.

Techniques

The techniques used for cold porcelain are very similar to those used in sugarcraft. The only real difference is that you cannot soften the edge of petals on foam pads with a dog bone tool. This rips the edge of the petal. We prefer to use metal ball tools; using a rolling rather than a dragging action.

Softening the Edges of Petals or Leaves

Place the petal or leaf on the foam pad. With the ball half on and half off the petal or leaf, roll a ball tool around the edge. This should create a soft wave. The more gentle the effect you want to achieve, the larger size ball you should use. Once this has been mastered, you may prefer to use it for sugarwork as well!

Frilling

Petals can be frilled with the Holly Products Ceramic Silk Veining Tool. Place the petal on your non-stick board and roll the tool over the petal. This can be done repeatedly until the degree of frilling required is achieved. The same method can be applied using blunt cocktail sticks or the small CelStick. When frilling the edge of a petal it is best to frill both sides as there is a tendency for the worked edge of the petals to curl up slightly. By frilling both sides of the petal this curling is prevented. Some petals actually have this slight curling on the edges so for them just frill one side.

A softer, more dramatic frill can be achieved on the edge of a petal or leaf using frilling sticks of different thicknesses. Place the section of the petal to be frilled along the edge of your forefinger. Hold the frilling stick between the finger and thumb of the working hand. Place the frilling stick onto the petal with the working hand beyond the hand holding the petal and work the petal. The depth into the petal of the frill can be controlled by how far onto the petal the stick goes. By dropping the height of the working hand and lifting the tip of the frilling stick off the petal you can frill just the very edge of the petal. This may sound awkward, but with a little practice this technique is quickly mastered.

Curling the edges of petals must be done with caution; cold porcelain shrinks as it dries so any curl you make becomes tightened. If you do make a mistake and over-curl a petal so that when it is dried it touches its back this can be corrected by using steam or a hairdryer to soften the cold porcelain so you can create a more gentle curl. Any petal or leaf that has dried in a strange shape can also be warmed again and re-shaped.

Hints, Tips and Advice

Apply a slight smear of cold cream to the edge of the cutters to prevent the paste from sticking to them. Keep a toothbrush handy to brush off any tiny pieces which may still adhere.

It is important to remember to dust the surface of the cold porcelain lightly with cornflour before using a template otherwise it may stick.

Always dust double veiners with cornflour as the cold porcelain sticks very easily. Once the cold porcelain has stuck to a veiner do not try to persevere. Wash the veiner, dry it well, dust with cornflour and try again. When first using a new veiner it sometimes helps to rub a little cold cream onto them, removing it very carefully with kitchen paper before dusting with cornflour. Veiners which are used on a regular basis do not often stick.

Use white covered wires for inserting into both petals and leaves. The shrinkage of the paste makes the green covered wires very obvious.

You do not have to use a grooved board when making leaves. Roll the paste thicker than usual where the wire is to be inserted. Vein the leaf with the double veiner, place the leaf on a foam pad and use a cocktail stick to deepen the central vein where the wire is to be inserted. Moisten the wire with thinned down glue and press it firmly into the grooved central vein and then pinch the leaf around the wire carefully from the back of the leaf. Ensure that you have a good seal around the wire. When the cold porcelain dries it will shrink and any gap will widen. Use a little softened cold porcelain to fill the gap and smooth with a moistened finger.

A small hook on the end of a white wire inserted into the base of a petal is sufficient in cold porcelain. If you prefer to make your petals or leaves with the wires inserted far up the petal or leaf you may continue to do this, but the shrinkage of the paste does mean there is a greater likelihood of the wire being exposed if inserted this way. Adjust the thickness of your paste to prevent exposure of the wire.

It takes experimentation to grow accustomed to the element of shrinkage common to all cold porcelain. Different brands shrink by greater or lesser amounts. Freshly-made cold porcelain shrinks more than paste which is a little more mature. The shrinkage of cold porcelain has elements of both comedy and tragedy. Always allow a great deal of time when making animals or figures. Allow weeks rather than days. Each thinly applied layer should be completely dry before you add the next or you will not be able to control the final shape. When making heads, figures, animals and birds it is advisable to use Asi-es paste rather than a home-made paste as you can (providing you have some of your starting colour) add wet Asi-es paste to dry paste, smooth it with water and once dry again, you will not be able to see the join. You must get into the habit of keeping small pieces of coloured paste in appropriately marked bags for just such an emergency. It is extremely difficult to try to match colours later as the colour deepens as it dries.

If this drying time has not been allowed during the making of a piece you will be absolutely amazed at the change in the piece after a few months. When Tombi first made a figure (a bride), a long time was spent carving and smoothing the face until it looked beautiful. When it was removed from its box three months later, it had shrunk by an amazing extent and had to be built up again!

Making hands to go with a figure can be quite tricky as the thicker the paste is the longer it takes to dry out and hands that were in proportion with a figure when it was made can later appear to be completely wrong. This applies to noses, lips and ears on heads too!

African Violets
(Saintpaulia)

There are many varieties of African violets, with single or double, wavy or ruffled flowers in white and shades of pink, red, purple and blue, as well as bi-coloured flowers and miniatures. This plant originated in Tanzania, and the more attractive types can be made as a delightful present to give to a loved one, although it may be a good idea to make a pretty label which remains attached to the pot saying 'Please don't water'!

TP

Materials

Cold porcelain with some Permanent White gouache added: pale Sap Green, yellow and burgundy (a blend of Deep Magenta, Brilliant Violet and Burnt Sienna)

Gouache: Permanent White, Sap Green, Primary Yellow, Deep Magenta, Brilliant Violet and Burnt Sienna

Craft dust: Sap Green, Jade, Burnt Sienna, black, yellow, Deep Magenta, burgundy, purple, Permanent Rose and dark green (a blend of Sap Green, Jade, Burnt Sienna and black)

Oil paints: Windsor Violet, Permanent Rose, Magenta, Crimson Alizarin, Cadmium Red (deep hue) Titanium White, Sap Green, Chrome Green, and black

Oil painting thinners with paint drying liquid added

28 and 26 gauge white wire

20 and 18 gauge wire

White floristry tape

Attractive pot

Florists' Staysoft

Fine model railway gravel in various colours, mixed together

Matt spray varnish

Equipment

Great Impressions African Violet leaf veiners or home-made veiners

Orchard Products cutters Nos. F9 and 10

Tinkertech Two smallest Calyx cutter No. 406

Tinkertech Two smallest Simple Leaf cutter No. 229, compressed so it is narrower

Fine palette knife

Buds

1. Make a large number of round balls in varying sizes and stick them onto 28 gauge wires with PVA glue.

2. Roll out white porcelain paste and using the F10 cutter, cut out blossom shapes. Soften the edges of the petal shapes on a Billy's block. Moisten the balls one at a time with a little water. Cover the smallest balls with just two petals, the slightly larger ones with three petals and the largest balls with all five petals.

3. Roll out the burgundy paste until fine. Using the small calyx cutter cut out calyxes from the burgundy paste and fasten them behind the buds centring the sepals between the petals.

Stamens

1. Moisten the end of a 26 gauge wire with a little PVA glue. Make four tiny equal-sized balls of yellow paste. Make them into cone shapes and stick them around the wire, points down, so you have four yellow, rounded stamens attached to the wire. When they are dry paint them with a little diluted oil paint or dust with yellow craft dust.

2. Roll a fine cone of white paste and stick this onto the wire, pointing up alongside the stamens. Set aside to dry.

Single Flowers

1. Finger out a small piece of white paste leaving a slightly thickened piece of paste in the centre. Roll out the paste from the thickened centre. The paste should be rolled thinner on one side.

2. Cut out a petal shape with the F10 cutter, positioning two petal shapes over the thinner part of the paste.

3. Elongate the three thicker petals by rolling the paste outwards with a CelStick. The central petal is longer than the other two.

4. Broaden these petals by rolling a CelStick sideways from the centre of the petal to the outer edge, making sure you keep an attractive shape. The central petal of the three is the broadest.

5. Place the flower on the Billy's block and soften the edges of all five petals. Cup very gently by rolling a ball tool from the edge towards the centre of the flower.

6. Press the point of a small CelStick into the centre of the flower. Apply a little glue and thread the wire of a prepared set of stamens through the centre of the flower, arranging the white spike between the two small petals. Set the flower aside to dry.

7. Make some of the flowers with the petals cupped together to represent an opening bud.

8. Make a few larger flowers either by stretching the petals or by using the larger cutter.

9. Add burgundy calyxes, positioning the sepals between the petals.

Double Flowers

1. Roll out a piece of white paste, fairly fine. Cut out a number of blossom shapes using the F10 cutter. Cover them with a plastic mat to keep them moist.

2. Gently vein and enlarge each petal with a ceramic silk veining tool. Lift the blossom and work the edge of the petal on your finger using a petal frilling tool.

3. Place on a foam pad and cup each petal with a metal ball tool. This will remove the excessive veining from the petal.

4. Moisten the centre of the blossom with glue and thread through the prepared stamens. Hang upside down to dry.

5. The second layer of petals is a repeat of the process for the first layer but using the larger cutter.

6. Arrange the second layer of petals across the junctions of the first layer.

7. Add burgundy calyxes, positioning the sepals between the petals.

8. For both single and double flowers, before the flowers are completely dry dust them appropriately. Some flowers just have a little colour on the edges of the petals, some are almost white around the stamens deepening the colour towards the edge of the petal. Choose the type of finish you want. If you can, have an actual plant next to you when you are dusting. Notice how the flowers change colour as they age and recreate this effect in your plant.

9. Tape the buds and flowers into groups of two with the odd group of three; using quarter to third-width white floristry tape. Each time you tape a pair of buds or flowers together cut the top of the tape in half lengthways; leave a $^1/_4$ inch sticking up. Trim to the shape of tiny bracts. Vary the height of the buds and flowers in these groups. Small buds have the shortest stalks, lengthening as they grow into flowers. Tape these groups into a cluster of about fifteen flowers and buds making sure they are of different heights. Paint the stems and tiny bracts burgundy to match the calyxes.

Bracts

1. Using a fine groove, roll out some pale green paste.

2. Moisten a 28 gauge wire with a little glue and position along the groove about a third of the length of the simple leaf cutter. Press the wire into the paste in the groove using your rolling pin. Fold the rolled-out green paste back over the wire to the end of the board and roll out the paste once again until it is fairly fine. Cut out the bract using the simple leaf cutter. Place on Billy's block and soften the edges of the bract. Make a pair of bracts for each group of flowers and buds. Dust them with Sap Green dust. Leave the underside pale green.

3. Fasten a pair of bracts immediately below a cluster of buds and flowers.

Leaves

1. Make templates from the veiners.

2. Make the leaves by repeating the process for making the bracts; use the medium and large grooves and 20 and 18 gauge wires. The wires need to be such a heavy gauge as less heavy wires will bend into unattractive shapes when pushed into the Staysoft.

3. Cut out the leaf shapes using the templates; dust the rolled-out paste with cornflour before placing the template on the paste as paste tends to stick to cardboard; leave a $^1/_4$ to 1 inch of paste below the cut-out leaf for the stalks.

4. Dust the veiner with cornflour. Place the cut-out leaf into the veiner with the ridge resting in the groove. Press firmly. Remove from the veiner.

5. Place the leaf on the Billy's block with the upper surface of the leaf against the pad. Take the small metal ball tool and using a pulling, scooping action create scallops along the edges of the leaves. Roll the ball tool around the edge of the leaf to soften the scalloping slightly and to give some movement to the edges of the leaf.

6. Lift the leaf and roll the paste below the leaf into a neat round stalk. Gently pinch the leaf along the central back vein to accentuate it. Use the smooth end of the metal veining tool to curve the edges of the leaves near the tip. Bend the wire in the stalks into a graceful curve with the leaf itself at a slight angle from the stalk. Set aside to firm slightly.

7. Before the paste is completely dry dust the leaves. Decorate the underside of the leaves first. Carefully paint or dust burgundy craft dust onto the surface of the leaves leaving the pale green veins exposed. Paint or dust the leaf stalks burgundy with some green showing through. If you have used dust seal the underside of the leaf with matt varnish and allow to dry before decorating the upper surface of the leaves. Paint the leaf dark green, dust over dark green then a small amount of burgundy. Leave the leaf looking as velvety as possible. Set aside to dry. Seal the leaf with matt varnish.

Note: Some African violet leaves have smooth edges. If you choose to make that variety then there is no need to scallop the edges of the leaves, just soften them. Others not only have scalloped edges but have frilled edges as well; after scalloping the edges use the frilling stick on your finger to frill the edges of the petals before curving them over the frilling stick. Some white African violets have only small, bright green leaves. With this variety the stems and calyxes of the buds and flowers are also pale green. Choose the leaf finish to suit the variety of your flower.

Assembly

1. Fill the chosen plant pot with Staysoft. Cover the Staysoft with a little PVA glue and sprinkle the model train gravel over it to resemble soil.

2. Push the leaves into the Staysoft. To get the best result copy the leaf grouping from a real plant. The small leaves grow in clusters with the larger leaves surrounding these small leaves.

3. Insert the flower clusters into the centre of the cluster of leaves. Some smaller varieties of flowers are arranged just above or among the leaves, but the larger, bolder flowers are arranged proud of the leaves. They can be arranged as just one plant in a pot or in several clusters to represent more than one plant in a pot. If you do this you can dust your leaves differently and assemble the different colours in different clusters and colour the flowers to go with the leaves thus having several distinct plants in one pot. Single and double plants can be arranged next to one another in one pot.

Flowering Currant
(Ribes sanguineum - 'King Edward VII')

This plant is very attractive to look at but has an extremely unpleasant smell. It is not often used in arrangements for this reason. However, in cold porcelain the problem of smell is eliminated, so it is a delightful plant to use in a suitable arrangement.

Three spays of ribes have been used in the camellia arrangement, each having two clusters of flowers and a good number of leaves.

TP

Materials

Cold Porcelain with Permanent White gouache added

Cold porcelain coloured pale green using Sap Green gouache.

Craft dust: Scarlet and Sap Green

Sugarcraft dust: Vine

30, 28, 26, and 20 gauge white wires

Tiny white seed-head stamens

Nile Green floristry tape

Diluted Anita's Semi-gloss découpage varnish

Matt varnish spray

Equipment

Great Impressions small and medium Hop Leaf veiners

3 sizes of dendrobium orchid tongue cutters

Sugar Celebrations tiny Calyx cutter No. SC73

Buds

1. Take a tiny piece of paste, moisten the end of a quarter-length 30 gauge wire and insert it into the paste. Form a tiny pointed bud with a well marked neck and a long, fine tube. Make these in three or four sizes, but all of them should be very small.

2. Dust the buds lightly with Scarlet craft dust and at the junction between the paste and the wire give the bud a dash of green to represent the minute calyx.

Flowers

1. Take a 30 gauge wire and stick five very short tiny seed-head stamens to the wire in a cluster.

2. Make a Mexican hat of paste with a very fine tube, place the cutter over the tube, cut it out. Elongate each petal slightly (this will also make them fine). Lift the flower and gently indent each petal with the fine frilling stick. Open the throat with the frilling stick.

3. Moisten the base of the stamens with a little glue and pull into the neck of the flower. Roll the tube between your fingers to get a good join and taper the tube gently.

4. Before the paste is completely dry gently dust the flower with Scarlet craft dust being careful not to get it on the stamens or on the flower immediately surrounding the stamens. Dust a little green onto the base of the tube to represent the calyx. Spray the flowers and buds with matt varnish.

Leaves

1. Make the leaves in three sizes, using wires of suitable gauge for the size of the leaf.

2. Roll a long sausage of paste, roll away from the sausage with your rolling pin leaving a ridge of thicker paste from which to cut the base of the leaves.

3. Insert the wires into the thickened paste after moistening the wires with a little glue.

4. Dust the veiner with cornflour and vein the leaf.

5. Remove from the veiner, place the leaf on the board and serrate and frill the edge of the leaf using the dresden tool. Remember to work both sides of each leaf.

6. Reinforce the central vein by pinching the leaf from the back, cut off the unwanted paste from the square ends of the cutter if they are very obvious.

7. Set the leaves aside to dry.

8. Before the leaves are completely dry dust them. The tiny leaves are dusted with Vine sugarcraft dust. The edges of the larger leaves are dusted with this colour as well, and then the larger leaves are overdusted with Sap Green craft dust. The larger the leaf the more Sap Green is added.

9. Dip the leaves into diluted Anita's varnish.

Assembly

Tape groups of buds into clusters ensuring the buds are different lengths. Tape these groups together so you get a spray of buds of increasing length and width. Tape the flowers into groups making sure that they too are different lengths; tape these into the spray. Tape these onto a 20 gauge wire. Add the tiny leaves then the larger leaves, alternating and spiralling the leaves down the stem. Now tape two sprays together, ensuring they are different lengths as well. Tape small groups of three, five and seven leaves together and tape these to the 20 gauge wires below the taped sprays.

Twigs

*T*wigs *make very good background material for arrangements, they are much quicker and easier to make than an equivalent sized piece of greenery.* **TP**

Materials

28, 26, 24, 20 and 18 gauge wires

Twig floristry tape

Method

For the fine twigs use quarter-width tape. Tape a 28 gauge wire, leaving about 1 inch of tape beyond the wire.

Use a fine pair of scissors to cut this tape lengthways. Rub your finger and thumb briskly on a full piece of tape. Twist the fine pieces of tape until they form threads.

The larger the twig, the heavier and longer the wire and the broader the tape. The process is the same.

Assembly

Using half-width tape now begin to add the fine twigs to 24 gauge wires, these in turn are taped to 20 gauge wires which in turn are taped onto the main 18 gauge wire. Make each branch of twigs as large or small as you need it to be.

Camellia
(Camellia reticulata 'Balderdash')

*E*ven if I hadn't liked
the look of this camellia
it might well have been
the one I chose to make - just for the name itself. 'Balderdash!'
was an expletive I heard from my father from my earliest
years - it is expressive, rounded and mellifluous if said
correctly! The colour of my flowers are a little bolder, but have
kept the narrow, not very curved leaves. Another thing I like
about camellias is the description of their leaves. They have
serrulate margins - 'serrulate' - another wonderful word!

TP

Materials

Cold porcelain with Permanent White gouache added

Cold Porcelain coloured pale green with Sap Green gouache

Craft dust: yellow, Deep Magenta, Scarlet, Sap Green, Jade, Burnt Sienna and dark green (a blend of Sap Green, Jade, Burnt Sienna and black)

Sugarcraft dust: Vine, Holly/Ivy and black

26, 24 and 20 gauge white wires

18 gauge green wires

Large seed-head stamens (yellow with white filaments)

Nile Green and Twig floristry tape

Diluted Anita's Semi-gloss découpage varnish

Matt and satin spray varnish

Equipment

Great Impressions very large Rose Petal veiner

Great Impressions Camellia Leaf veiners

Tinkertech Two cutters, broad side petals of cattleya orchids (3 sizes)

Tinkertech Two large Rose Petal cutters Nos. 549 - 551

Orchard Products Five Petal Flower cutters Nos. F6A, F7 and F8

Cardboard apple tray cups cut apart into neat cups, small and large

'Magic' tape

Kitchen paper

Buds

1. On a 20 gauge wire make a blunt cone of paste, similar to that of a rose but with a more rounded tip and not as tall.

2. Roll out a piece of paste, cut out several shapes using the F6A, F7 and F8 cutters. Place them under the plastic mat to keep them moist.

3. Place one shape cut with the F6A cutter onto the foam pad and soften the edge with the metal ball tool.

4. Apply a little glue to the centre of the shape, push the cone wire through the centre of the shape, sticking the petals over the cone creating a bud. The petals do not have to spiral. Repeat this process with a second layer, allowing these petals to unfurl slightly. Remember to place the petal of the second layer over the joins of the first layer.

5. Make the calyx using two layers of the shapes cut with the F8 cutter, remembering to place the sepals of the second layer over the joins of the first.

6. Before the paste is completely dry dust the bud with Deep Magenta and Scarlet. Dust the edge of the sepals with a little Vine and then dust over it from the wire with Holly/Ivy and then with Sap Green. Once the paste is completely dry carefully spray the petals with matt varnish and the sepals with satin varnish. Mask the other pieces with kitchen paper and 'Magic' tape.

Flowers

1. Bend a circle at the top of an 18 gauge wire, bend it at a 90 degree angle and then centre the wire behind the hole. Dip the circle in glue and stick a small ball of green paste into the circle. Open a hole into the green paste with a CelStick. Set aside to dry.

2. Take a bunch of large seed-head stamens. Divide them into five groups. Apply tacky glue to the stamens and squeeze the glue firmly up the filaments of the stamens until they are all stuck to one another. Cut the stamens the length you need them for the flower you are making. Add glue to the green paste around the circle bent into the wire. Stick the glued-together stamens all the way around this centre. The stamens in a camellia are rather straight and neat. Use all the stamens in this way spreading them evenly around the

circle. This circle in the centre of a camellia is one of its more notable feature. Dust the anthers with yellow craft dust.

3. Use the smallest of the three large rose petal cutters for making five inner petals. Roll the paste thicker at the end where you will have the pointed end of the cutter. Cut out five petals. Keep them under the plastic mat until you can work them.

4. Cut five 24 gauge wires into threes and hook them. Moisten the hook with glue and slide it into the thickened paste at the pointed end of the petal. Dust the rose petal veiner with cornflour and vein the petal. Soften the edge of the petal by working the petal over your finger with a fine metal frilling tool. Arrange the petal in a small apple cup with the frilled edge over the side. You must be very careful that you have a smooth line where the wire goes into the petal. Any awkward shapes here will make it very difficult to assemble the flower. Repeat this process for all five petals in the inner layer.

5. Use the largest of the rose petal cutters to make a further ten petals to complete the flower. Repeat the process described above, only using the medium frilling stick on the edges of the petals. Frill very lightly or the petals may become over-frilled. This is not too much of a problem as there are frilly varieties as well, but 'Balderdash' is only moderately frilled. Curl several of these petals more than the others. They will go in the outer layer.

6. When the petals are almost dry dust them first with Scarlet craft dust and then add the Deep Magenta. If you brush gently sideways with the Deep Magenta it will emphasise the veining on the petals.

Assembling the Flower

1. Use a pair of pliers to bend the wires of the petals as you tape them in place with the half-width Twig floristry tape. The petals are not in a precise order, nor do they spiral. Gradually add the larger petals; the look of the flower is improved if the odd petal is pulled in front of petals that have already been taped in. It gives the flower a less formal appearance. The more curled petals should be taped into the outer layer.

2. Make the calyx using two layers of cold porcelain cut from green paste with the F7 cutter, softened on the foam pad and stuck to the outer petals of the flower. The second layer goes over the joins of the first layer. Dust the edges of the calyx with a little Vine dust, then bring in Holly/Ivy from the wire inwards and then an overdusting of Sap Green. Spray the flower with matt varnish. The calyx should be sprayed with satin varnish after the back of the petals have been masked.

Leaves

1. Roll out paste over a medium groove, moisten a 26 gauge wire, press it into the paste in the groove taking the wire about two thirds of the way up the leaf. Cut out the leaf using the smallest size cutter.

2. Remove the leaf from the groove. Place the leaf, ridge up, on the board and with an angled craft knife nick out small wedges of paste to make the serrulations on the margin of the leaf.

3. Place the leaf on the foam pad and soften the edge gently.

4. Dust the veiner with cornflour and place the leaf on the veiner with the ridge in the groove. Vein the leaf. Remove the leaf and give it a little movement. Set the leaf on dimpled foam to dry.

5. Repeat this process until you have many leaves in different sizes. When the leaves are almost dry dust them with a dark green mixture, overdusted with Sap Green. The small leaves should first be dusted with Vine and then overdusted with Sap Green. Dip the leaves into very slightly diluted Anita's varnish. Set aside to dry.

Assembly

Cut 20 gauge wires in half. Use half-width Twig floristry tape bound over the end of the cut wire to represent a growth bud. Add three, five and seven leaves to these wires. Some should be of young, bright leaves. Wire these groups of leaves to buds and flowers, but keep some just to add as foliage. You can never have too many leaves.

Camellia Arrangement

*U*nfortunately I have no floristry training. At home
any flowers I receive are pushed higgledy-piggledy
into a large square slab pot made by my mother. It is
more usual to find flowers in my fridge than on any
usual surface. I create arrangements that I feel look
attractive.

TP

Flowers

Assortment of twigs

3 sprays of ribes

3 camellia flowers

2 camellia buds

Equipment

Oval bonsai dish

Florists' green Staysoft

Method

Make an oval ball of paste in the centre of the dish. It will need to be large enough to hold all items to be used in the arrangement, but if too large it requires a lot of work to disguise it. Create the outline of the arrangement with your twigs. Once these are in place it should flow more easily. Re-emphasise the outline with the sprays of ribes.

Add the focal point flower and then the two subsidiary flowers. The flower behind the focal point is smaller than the other two. Add foliage if any Staysoft is visible. Stand back from the arrangement and study it from all angles. Look for any ugly space, or where items may be too crowded together. Make any final adjustments until you are happy with the arrangement, although it is important not to work on it for too long, as it can lose 'soul'.

Gloxinia
(Sinningia)

*T*he ancestor of our modern sinningia hybrid is **Sinningia Speciosa**. It grows in southern Brazil on damp, rocky slopes, producing dainty, violet-blue flower bells. In l815 the plant was taken to England where it was hybridised.

This flower has been chosen as another plant in a pot as the same veiner is used to make the leaves as is used for the African violet. The veiners are expensive to buy so it is advisable to be able to use them for more than one plant or flower. To make an attractive display you can make more than one plant for your pot. Each plant should consist of three buds of different sizes, an opening flower and at least two fully open flowers, plus approximately sixteen leaves.

TP

Materials

Cold porcelain with Permanent White gouache added

Gouache: Permanent White

Craft dust: yellow (dilute some yellow with white craft dust so you have a pale yellow dust), Scarlet, Permanent Rose, Deep Magenta, Sap Green, Jade, Burnt Sienna, black and dark green (a blend of Sap Green, Jade, Burnt Sienna and black)

Sugarcraft dust: Edelweiss, Aubergine and burgundy

Oil paints: yellow, Magenta, Permanent Rose, Sap Green, Terre Verte, Cadmium Red (deep hue), black and Titanium White

Thinners with paint drying liquid added

28, 26, 24 and 22 gauge white wires

20 and 14 gauge green or uncovered wires

Large white seed-head stamens

Nile Green floristry tape

Attractive pot

Florists' Staysoft

Model train gravel in various colours to represent soil

Matt spray varnish

Equipment

Tinkertech Two Six Petal Blossom cutters in varying sizes

Orchard Products Six Petal Flower cutters Nos. N4, N5, and N6

Great Impressions African Violet veiners

Pistil and Stamens

1. Take a small piece of white paste, roll it into a ball and then a cone shape. Moisten the end of a piece of 20 gauge wire with a little glue. Push the dry end of the wire into the thick end of the cone and work the moistened piece of wire into the cone ending just below the broadest piece of paste.

2. Roll the piece of paste onto the wire with your fingers and then roll between the outer edges of your palms to remove the finger marks.

3. Pinch the protruding piece of paste into a fat disk at the top of the wire. Cut out small 'V' shapes from the disk giving you five or six points.

Supporting these small pieces of paste on your forefinger one at a time, spread the paste making a stigma with five or six rounded indentations.

4. Press the square end of a frilling stick into each piece to indent it. Set aside to dry.

5. Roll a small piece of green paste into a ball and cut in half. Moisten the wire just below the dry pistil with a little glue. Thread the half ball onto the wire with the flat side up. Nestle it just below the pistil.

6. Cut three stamens in half, removing about a $1/4$ inch from the centre to shorten the stamens. Using a needle tool, make evenly-spaced holes in the hemisphere.

7. Curve the stamens using your pliers or tweezers.

8. Moisten the filament of the stamen with a little glue and push them into the ready-made holes. Arrange the stamens so they curve towards the pistil.

9. The anthers should come just below the stigma. The colour of the anthers is determined by the colour of the flower chosen. Either use a good flower book or a real flower to establish the correct colour for the flower you are making. The flower copied here had pale yellow anthers. Paint the stamens with a little pale yellow oil paint and then apply the pale yellow craft dust. Be careful not to get yellow on the stigma or style as in most flowers these appear to be creamy white.

Buds

1. Take a 20 gauge wire and cut it into three. Use your pliers to form a small circle at the end of one wire. Bend this to a 90 degree angle from the wire. If you want to perfect it, bend the wire so that it emerges from the centre of the circle like an old-fashioned ski stick.

2. Make a small ball of paste (for small buds the paste should be pale green, becoming more white as the buds get larger) and form it into a very shallow, pointed cone. Moisten the ski stick

and insert it into the flat part of the cone.

3. Use a sharp pair of scissors to trim the edges of the cone to form a hexagon at the base. Carefully pinch the cone from the points of the hexagon to the tip of the cone. Moisten your finger and smooth over the ridges to achieve a pretty, smooth bud which has this attractive hexagonal shape at the base. Set aside until almost dry and then dust the buds.

4. Larger buds can be covered with six petal blossom shapes cut flat, with the edges of the petals softened. The junctions between the petals should match the corners of the hexagon. Once again dust these buds.

5. Roll out mid-green paste and cut shapes for your calyxes. Match the size of the calyx to your bud, bearing in mind the shrinkage factor. Work each sepal on your finger using a fine frilling stick. Each sepal is shaped like the prow of a boat. Moisten the centre of the calyx with glue and pull a bud into the calyx, positioning the sepals at the points of the hexagon.

6. Dust the calyx using various greens and some burgundy and Aubergine if copying the one in the book. The sepals are slightly paler on the inside than on the outside. Spray with matt varnish.

Flowers

1. Take a fairly large piece of paste, form into a sausage shape with a rounded end; flatten the other end into a circle enlarging it so that it is almost large enough to accommodate the cutter chosen. Use a medium CelStick or something similar to roll out the paste, ensuring that you have a good 90 degree angle between the tube and the petals. Cut out the blossom shape.

2. Use a cocktail stick to work each petal. Work from the centre of a petal, frilling and shaping each petal carefully so an oval petal shape is retained, but enlarging them so that they overlap one another. Be careful not to join the petals together while you are frilling them, and not to

stretch the paste between the petals.

3. Lift the flower and frill the edges of the petal firmly on your finger with a fine frilling stick so the edges become very ruffled.

4. Very carefully open the tube using the pointed end of a large CelStick. Insert the rounded end into the tube and ensure you have a rounded curved base to the flower.

5. You must ensure that two petals immediately opposite one another are arranged on top of the other four petals. The petals of a gloxinia always open in opposing pairs.

6. Some gloxinias have mottled or spotted decorations in the base of their trumpets. To achieve this you must make a small hole in the base of the trumpet and set the flower aside to dry until it is firm enough to take the handling necessary for this painting process. Once the flower is firm enough to handle, decorate the inside.

7. Moisten the base of the flower centre with glue and carefully pull it into the flower. If the flower is dry it is worth softening the base of the tube over steam so that the two pieces fit neatly together.

8. Using a little oil paint mixed to the colour you want and just a touch of thinner, very carefully paint the inside of the flower brushing the colour onto the petals. The gloxinia copied did not have a mottled throat but was paler at the base of the trumpet. The colour did not reach the ruffled edges of the petals and the back of the flower was white. Very carefully dust over the oil paints giving a velvety look to the petals. Using Edelweiss sugarcraft dust, dust the edges and back of the flower with extreme care. Allow to dry. Spray with matt varnish. Allow to dry before adding the calyx.

9. Make the calyx as described for the bud, positioning the sepals between the petals.

10. Dust the calyx. Spray with matt varnish.

Leaves

1. The leaves grow in opposite pairs, spiralling down the stem and increasing in size. The flowers and buds emerge from the leaf axils. Large, medium and small leaves are made the same way, using finer wires and smaller grooves as the leaves reduce in size.

2. Make templates from the leaf veiners.

3. To make a large leaf roll out some white paste over a large groove in your grooved board rolling the paste to a long tongue beyond the groove. Moisten a 22 gauge white wire and stick it onto the paste over the groove. You need the wire to be long enough to go two thirds of the way up the leaf, remembering that the leaf stalk also needs to have paste on it. Press the wire into the paste with your rolling pin. Fold down the tongue of paste over the wire to the end of the board. Roll out again. The wire is now embedded between two layers of paste.

4. Dust the surface of the paste with cornflour and position the template onto the paste leaving enough paste below the template for the leaf stalk. Cut out the shape.

5. Dust the veiner, place the ridge of paste into the groove in the leaf and press the veiners together. Carefully separate them. Use your fingers to remove the mark left by the veiner at the base of the leaf. With a frilling stick, gently re-emphasise the central vein. Place the leaf's upper surface onto your Billy's block and use the small ball tool in a scooping, pulling movement to create a gently scalloped edge to the leaf; carefully soften the edge of the leaf stalk. Position the leaf over your finger and use your frilling stick to flute the edges of the leaves. Bend the leaf to an attractive shape, support and allow to dry.

6. When the leaves are almost dry paint them using Sap Green and Terre Verte oil paints with a minute amount of black added, mixed with a tiny amount of thinners; the edges of the leaf stalk are also green. Leave the central vein creamy white. Paint the underside of the leaf a paler green

than the top. Dust the upper surface of the leaf with Sap Green and dark green mixture. Once the leaves are dry, spray with matt varnish.

Assembly

1. Fill the pot with Staysoft, moisten the upper surface with PVA glue and spread with the 'soil'.

2. Select a 14 gauge wire, and with half-width floristry tape bind the wire at the top several times to create a small growth bud. Fold about $2/3$ inch floristry tape back on itself just below this 'growth bud', pinch it together firmly, fold in the upper edges to form a point, twist firmly and push this leaflet against the side of the stem partly enclosing the bud. Repeat this again on the other side of the stem so you have a pair of small leaflets enclosing the bud. Tape down a further $1/2$ inch and repeat this process making another pair of slightly larger leaflets, emerging just below and between the first pair.

3. Tape the first pair of small cold porcelain leaves onto the wire, allowing them to be quite close together and enveloping the previous two stages. Add another pair of small leaves about $1/2$ inch below the first pair and then a third pair, keeping them opposite one another but spiralling them down the stem. Cut away the excess wire. Add buds and flowers to the stem adding a leaf immediately behind them and remembering to wire in the opposing leaf as well. When you have added all the elements you have made, measure the stem against the depth of the pot and cut away any excess wire there may be. Neaten the tape by rubbing with the back of the blade of a pair of large scissors. Dust the stem to look realistic. The colour is lighter towards the top of the stem. Using a broad brush paint over the dusted stem with PVA glue. Allow to dry. Using a pair of pliers to hold the stem, force the wire into the bottom of the pot. Arrange the leaves, buds and flowers attractively. Repeat this process if you want more than one stem of flowers in the same pot. Remember to vary the height of the stems.

Maranta

Marantas are often known as prayer plants because of the way their young leaves fold together in the evening. There are many hybrid forms of this attractive foliage plant, with several having ornate markings and strong red veins. The variety pictured is one of the simpler to make in cold porcelain. They are useful for arrangements and bouquets because of their size and interesting markings.

AD

Materials

Cold porcelain: Sap Green

Gouache: Sap Green and Oxide of Chromium

Craft dust: red, Deep Magenta and dark green (a blend of Sap Green, Jade, Burnt Sienna and black)

Sugarcraft dust: Holly/Ivy and Aubergine

24, 22 and 20 gauge wire

Satin spray varnish

Equipment

Country Cutters Maranta Leaf cutters

1. Colour some cold porcelain to a pale green using Sap Green gouache. Roll out some paste leaving a thick ridge down the centre. Cut out a leaf shape using either one of the maranta cutters or free-hand with a sharp scalpel.

2. Moisten either a 24 or 22 gauge wire (depending upon the size of the leaf) and insert it into at least half the length of the leaf.

3. Place the leaf on a pad and soften the edges using the medium ball tool. Draw down a central vein on the leaf using the fine end of the dresden veining tool and then draw in some curved side veining.

4. Using a smaller ball tool, roll and cup each section between the veins to create the characteristic shaping that the leaf has. Curl the edges as required, remembering that the majority of the leaves of the plant are quite flat. Allow to dry.

Colouring

1. Dust the leaf with Holly/Ivy from the edges and then overdust slightly with the dark green mixture. Dust the back of the leaf with a mixture of Deep Magenta and red craft dust mixed with Aubergine sugarcraft dust. Introduce some of this colour onto the upper surface, especially at the base and at the tip.

2. Mix together some Sap Green and Oxide of Chromium gouache with a small amount of water to form an interesting strong green. Paint the detail veining using a fine paintbrush. Allow to dry. Glaze with a satin spray varnish. To use the leaves in a bouquet or arrangement you might have to strengthen the stem by adding another 22 or 20 gauge wire.

Calanthe Orchid
(Calanthe vestita)

The calanthe orchids are a genus which are very widespread. They were particularly sought after by the Victorians who often used them to decorate their houses at Christmas time. There is a white variety, as well as the more common one which has a pink to cerise tongue with the other two petals and the three sepals being white, just gently flushed with pink.

The flower shown and described here is not true to nature. It was 'hybridised' by me to suit an arrangement I had in mind. If you are wanting to produce a flower true to nature I would suggest you work from a botanical book. The alterations I have made are thus: I have reversed the bracts, making them increase in size down the stem, which makes the greenery heavier at the stem's base. I have altered the dorsal sepal to look like a third petal, and I have decreased the size and changed the shape of the buds.

TP

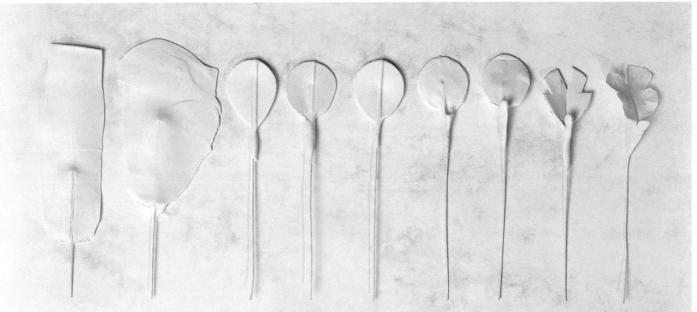

Materials

Cold Porcelain with Permanent White gouache added

Cold Porcelain coloured with Sap Green gouache

Craft dust: Sap Green and yellow

Sugarcraft dust: Vine

18 gauge wires

28, 26 and 24 gauge white wires

Nile Green floristry tape

Diluted Anita's Satin découpage varnish

Equipment

Tinkertech Two side petal of the Butterfly Orchid cutter No. 458

Tinkertech Two Rose Petal cutter No. 277

Tinkertech Two Simple Leaf cutters Nos. 225 - 228 and 230, 231, 232

Great Impressions Fine Orchid Petal veiner (old style) or Fine Poppy veiner (old style)

Flowers

1. Roll out a piece of white paste over a medium groove in your grooved board, rolling a long tongue. Moisten a third length 24 gauge white wire with glue and lay it along the groove. Press the wire into the groove with your rolling pin. Fold back the tongue of paste over the wire and roll the paste out again.

2. Place the rose petal cutter over the paste in the groove, about half an inch from the edge of the board with the pointed end aiming down

the wire. Press the cutter into the paste with your left hand. Hold the cutter in place and peel back the paste gently with your right hand. You should end up with paste left on the wire in the groove behind the pointed part of the cutter. Remove the cutter.

3. Lift the petal. Roll the extra paste into a throat for the orchid. If you do not have any paste left here add a small ball of paste immediately behind the petal and roll it into the throat. Cut an inverted 'V' shape out of the centre of the broad end of the petal and then cut two wedges, one from either side. The shape is similar to that of the epidendrum orchid, but larger.

4. Insert the small CelStick above the wire into the tube to form the throat. Roll a minute cone shape of paste and push this point first into the throat to form the column; once again use the CelStick to shape the column.

5. Trim the square edges of the petal to form nice rounded shapes and frill these petals with the silk veining tool. Pinch the back of the tongue to form a groove down the centre of the petal and then curve the tongue and its wire to an attractive shape.

6. The remaining five petals are made with the same cutter, but the wire is inserted from the different ends.

7. Use the grooved board to produce three sepals which are made by inserting the wire into the broad part of the cutter and two petals which are made by inserting the wire into the pointed end of the same cutter.

8. Dust the chosen veiner with cornflour and vein all five petals and sepals after the edges have been softened with a ball tool on a foam pad.

9. Gently run each of these pieces between your fingers to create a shallow groove in each piece and arrange over dimpled foam so that they will have attractive curves to them.

10. To assemble the orchid, tape the two lateral petals (round tips) on either side of the tongue, then tape in the three sepals (the dorsal sepal also has a rounded tip, the two lateral sepals have pointed tips). Bend the wire up behind the dorsal sepal and then back and down in a graceful curve.

11. Mould a small piece of paste into a cone shape. Moisten the junction of all the petals underneath the throat with a little glue and stick the blunt end of the cone shape onto the orchid (this forms a spur).

12. Curve the spur forward to make a graceful curve from below the base of the tongue.

Leaves

The leaves are made exactly the same way as the bracts, using the larger simple leaf cutters.

Assembly

You will need approximately five buds and three to five flowers to make up a good sized spray of orchids together with their bracts and about three to five leaves. In the bridal bouquet we have used three sprays of these orchids. The two shorter sprays each have three flowers and the larger spray has five flowers.

1. Use quarter-width Nile Green tape to tape short stems for the bracts and leaves.

2. Take an 18 gauge wire and tape a bud to the tip. Alongside this, tape in the bract. The buds and bracts are assembled alternately on either side of the wire. This same process is followed for the flowers as well. As the buds and flowers become larger the distance between the buds and flowers increases as well. The leaves are then taped on alternately. Dust the stem with Sap Green dust and paint with a layer of PVA glue. Bend the sprays of orchids into graceful curves.

13. Dust the base of the petals and sepals with a touch of Vine dust giving a lovely fresh greeny-white look to the orchid. With a very fine brush dust a little yellow dust just below the column on what would be the pollinium.

Buds

1. Cut 28 gauge wires into quarters and hook the wires.

2. Roll a cone-shaped piece of paste and roll the broad end to a slight point. Curve gently between your fingers.

3. Moisten the hook on a wire with glue and from the inside of the curve, about third way back on the bud insert the wire through the bud. Reverse the hooked end of the wire so it becomes imbedded in the broadest part of the bud. Use the small ball tool to close the hole made by the hook and make an attractive curve on the underside of the bud.

4. Mark the pointed, broad end of the bud to represent petals.

5. Dust the buds with a little Vine dust to give them a delicate greeny-white look. The smaller buds are greener than the larger buds.

Bracts

Each bud and flower has a bract.

1. Roll pale green paste over a small groove in your grooved board. Moisten a quarter length 28 gauge wire with glue and place on the paste in the groove. Press the wire into the paste with your rolling pin and fold back the tongue of paste to enclose the wire. Cut out the bract with the small leaf cutter. The larger buds and flowers have bigger bracts made using the larger cutters.

2. Soften the edge of the bract on the foam pad with the medium ball tool.

3. Vein strongly down the centre of the bract with the metal veining tool, being careful not to cut through the paste. Arrange on dimpled foam in an attractive shape and allow to dry.

4. When the bract is almost dry dust it with Sap Green craft dust, remembering that the underside of the bract is paler than the upper surface. Allow to dry completely and then dip the bract into the varnish.

Smilax

Smilax is a wonderful foliage plant that allows itself to be draped in large, graceful swags. It was used a great deal in Edwardian times to decorate the front of banqueting tables. It has, unfortunately, a very short growing season and is not readily available throughout the year but with cold porcelain we can remedy this!

TP

Materials

Cold porcelain with Permanent White gouache added, coloured green

Craft dust: Sap Green, Jade, Burnt Sienna and dark green (a blend of Sap Green, Jade, Burnt Sienna and black)

Sugarcraft dust: Holly/Ivy

30, 28 and 20 gauge wires

Dark green floristry tape

Diluted Anita's Semi-gloss découpage varnish

Equipment

Narrow side petal cutters from cattleya orchids (3 sizes)

Great Impressions Fine Orchid Petal veiner (old style) or corn-on-the-cob leaf

Method

1. Cut 30 gauge wires into fives, and 28 gauge wires into quarters.

2. Roll out a sausage of paste and roll the paste sideways from the sausage so you have paste which is thick at one end and thin at the other. Cut out the leaves with the rounded end of the cutters on the thicker paste.

3. Moisten the end of a 30 gauge wire with glue and insert it into the blunt, thicker end of the cut-out leaf shapes.

4. Dust the veiner and vein the leaf.

5. Run the leaf between your fingers, making a shallow groove lengthways down the leaf. Place on dimpled foam to set in gentle curves.

6. When the leaves are almost dry dust the smaller ones with Holly/Ivy sugarcraft dust then a thin layer of Sap Green craft dust from the base. The medium leaves should be dusted with Holly/Ivy sugarcraft dust at the tips, then overdusted with Sap Green from the wire, and then overdusted down the centre with some dark green mixture.

7. When the leaves are completely dry, dip them in the varnish and allow to dry.

Assembly

1. Tape the wire immediately below the leaves for a quarter to half an inch.

2. Tape the leaves into groups of three, five and seven onto 28 gauge wires. These in turn should be taped into larger groups on 24 gauge wires. Always having one leaf leading the leaf spray.

3. Tape these leaflets onto a 20 gauge wire until you have a foliage spray the right size for your needs.

Curved Bridal Bouquet

*T*his is a very popular shape for bridal bouquets, being quite easy for a bride to carry. This bouquet includes calanthe orchids, maranta leaves and smilax leaves as well as the ever popular rose; the finished effect is a transition between traditional and modern tastes.
AD

Flowers

3 large roses

4 rosebuds at various stages

1 long and two shorter stems of calanthe orchids

5 maranta leaves

7 stems of smilax

Equipment

18 gauge wires

Nile Green floristry tape

Fine pliers

Wire cutters

Candlestick for display

Preparation

1. Strengthen any of the flower stems that are very long or heavy, by taping in additional 18 gauge wires with half-width Nile Green floristry tape.

2. Decide how long you want the bouquet to be. The longest stem of calanthe orchids and smilax needs to measure approximately two thirds the length of the whole bouquet. Tape together the calanthe stem and a long stemmed smilax using half-width Nile Green floristry tape. Bend the stem to a 90 degree angle. Add the second longest stem of calanthe orchids with another stem of smilax to a length that will complete the remaining third of the length of the bouquet - again bend the stems to a 90 degree angle. Add the shortest stem of orchids and the remaining smilax to form the basic outline of the bouquet. You will need to make one side of the bouquet heavier to form the required curved shape, so you must make the stems at that side of the bouquet longer than at the other side.

3. Next tape in the largest or most attractive rose to the centre of the bouquet to form the focal point. This rose should stand higher than any of the other flowers in the arrangement. Tape the other two large roses at either side of the focal rose.

4. Use the rosebuds to emphasise the curved shape, placing the smaller buds at the very edges of the bouquet.

5. Finally add the maranta leaves to fill in the gaps in the design and any extra pieces of smilax that the bouquet needs. Neaten the handle of the bouquet using full-width Nile Green floristry tape. If the bouquet is to be carried by a bride then you will need to wrap the handle neatly with some satin ribbon to make it more comfortable to hold. The bouquet pictured has been displayed elegantly in a candlestick.

Sweet Violet
(Viola odorata)

This pretty little spring flower has been a source of great delight to many women over the centuries. The smell of violets always reminds me of my paternal grandmother who adored them. The prayerbook and silver cover were a Christmas present to my aunt, Phyllis, when she was four - from her parents! One wouldn't dream of giving a child a present of that nature for Christmas in this day and age!

TP

Materials

Cold Porcelain with Permanent White gouache added

Gouache: Sap Green and black

Craft dust: purple, Sap Green, Jade, Burnt Sienna and black

Sugarcraft dust: Plum, Edelweiss and black

28, 26 and 24 gauge white wire

Round, bright yellow stamens

Nile Green floristry tape

Diluted Anita's Semi-gloss découpage varnish

Matt spray varnish

Equipment

Great Impressions Violet Leaf veiners

Tinkertech Two heart-shaped cutters

Orchard Products Calyx cutter No. R15

Wooden skewer

Leaves

1. Colour some paste pale green with the Sap Green gouache.

2. Roll out a piece of paste over a medium groove. rolling a long tongue of paste.

3. Cut 26 gauge wires into three.

4. Moisten the end of a wire with glue and place it onto the paste in the groove. The wire should be two thirds the length of the leaf. Remember when making heart-shaped leaves you must leave more paste at the edge of the board than usual to accommodate the indentation. Fold back the paste and re-roll, trapping the wire between the two layers of paste. Cut out a leaf with a heart-shaped cutter.

5. Dust the veiner with cornflour. Place the cut-out leaf onto the veiner with the ridge in the groove. Press the veiners together and remove the leaf carefully. Place the leaf on a non-stick board. Use the dresden tool's sole to serrate the edge of the leaf by applying pressure and pulling away from the edge of the leaf.

6. Place the leaf on a Billy's block and soften the edge with a medium ball tool.

7. Place the leaf on dimpled foam to set. Make between fifteen and twenty leaves in varying sizes.

8. When the leaves are almost dry mix up some dark green craft dust using Sap Green, Jade, Burnt Sienna and a little black. Brush this dust onto the leaves using a flat brush. Use a circular motion. Dust a little Sap Green over the dark green from the edges. This lightens the edges slightly. The underside of the leaves should be paler than the upper surface.

9. When the leaves are dry dip them into the diluted glaze and set them aside to dry.

Buds

1. Take a very small piece of paste and roll into a blunt baton shape with a tapering back.

2. Use a cocktail stick to make an indentation on the bud about a third of the way from the tapered back.

3. Cut 26 gauge wires in half. Hook one end.

4. Moisten the hook with glue and pull the hook into the baton shape just in front of the indentation. Make sure the hole made by this process is sealed.

5. Using half-width floristry tape, tape the wire protruding from the bud.

6. Roll out some green paste and cut out a calyx with the R15 cutter. Split it between two sepals. Elongate the sepals on either side of the cut.

7. Apply a little glue to the bud just in front of where the wire protrudes and stick the sepals onto the bud with the sepals pointing towards the broad end.

8. Use a pair of fine nosed pliers to bend a graceful curve into the wire so the wire curves up and over the narrow end of the bud. Cut a 'V' shape into the end of a piece of tape and commence taping about halfway down the wire, leaving the points free. This represents the small bracts which grow on the stems of both the buds and the flowers.

9. Dust the bud delicately with the purple craft dust mixed with a little Plum sugarcraft dust. Dust a little Sap Green craft dust lightened with white to the rear of the bud, behind the calyx. Dust the calyx with Sap Green.

Flowers

1. Take a small piece of paste. Roll it into a ball and then into a cone shape.

2. Dip the wooden skewer into the cornflour and then push it firmly into the blunt end of the paste.

3. Very carefully cut the paste into three with a craft knife. Now cut two of the pieces in half. Remove the paste from the skewer. (If you prefer you can cut the paste with a pair of fine scissors - this method can give a heavier centre to the flower.)

4. Spread the five petals apart. Very carefully pinch the four narrower petals between your thumb and third finger.

5. Each petal must now be 'pulled'. Hold the whole petal between your thumb and your forefinger. The thumb must be at the top. Keep the thumb still and gently pull your forefinger along the length of the petal. This with both thin and curve the petal and give it a lovely rounded tip. Repeat this process for all five petals.

6. Place the large petal over the forefinger of your left hand and gently frill it with a blunt cocktail stick.

7. Pinch the underside of this petal to create a groove on the upper surface, and curve the petal gently downwards. The two middle petals may either be curved backwards or inwards, and the two top petals curve backwards.

8. Roll the thin end of the cone (which is behind the petals) to make it a good shape. It can become too blunt while you are working on the petals.

9. Tape a hooked wire with Nile Green tape. Dip the hook in glue. Pull the wire through the centre of the flower with the wire emerging at the back about third way from the point, behind the two upper petals.

10. Cut a bright yellow stamen very short and insert it into the centre of the flower.

11. Prepare the calyx as described for the bud and attach it to the back of the flower with the sepals coming forwards.

12. Bend the wire to a graceful curve as before.

13. Dust the flower with a mixture of purple craft dust and Plum sugarcraft dust, being careful to keep the centre of the flower white.

14. Mix a little black gouache with water and, using a very fine paintbrush, paint delicate black veins onto the three lower petals.

15. Spray the buds and flowers with matt varnish.

Bearded Iris
(Iris germanica hybrids)

The bearded iris has to be one of the most spectacular garden flowers. Unfortunately they tend to have quite a short flowering period. This cold porcelain alternative means that you can have bearded iris in a vase all year round if you wish. There are many species of iris and many more hybrid forms. It is best to have a flower or a photograph to copy for colour variations, petal shapes and detail markings. The iris has a rather grand history taking its name from the ancient Greek name for the messenger of the goddess Hera. Iris delivered messages to earth via the rainbow, which seems quite appropriate considering the vast range of colours the flower comes in. The iris was also the inspiration for the French fleur-de-lis.

AD

Materials

Cold porcelain: white and Sap Green

Craft dust: Sap Green, Deep Magenta, purple, yellow and dark green (a blend of Sap Green, Jade, Burnt Sienna and black)

Sugarcraft dust: Holly/Ivy, Vine, Daffodil, Lavender, Sunflower and Edelweiss

26 and 24 gauge white wire

22, 20 and 18 gauge wire

Nile Green floristry tape

Matt and satin spray varnish

Equipment

Asi-es Iris/Gladioli Cutting Sheet No. 3

Asi-es Orchid veiner No. 18

Dried sweetcorn husk veiner or Asi-es veiner No. 22

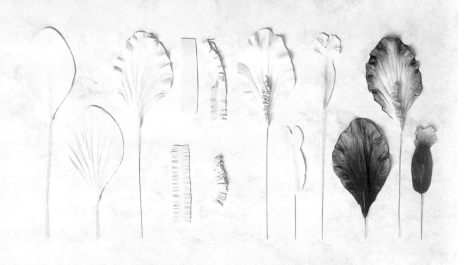

Outer Tepals (The Falls)

1. The three outer tepals (the 'falls') of the iris often hang downwards. They usually have distinctive markings down the centre, which can be in the form of a line of colour or in the case of the bearded iris, a furry beard! The size and the shape of the tepals vary between each of the varieties; here the gladioli cutter has been used to make a much larger flower-head. Roll out some white cold porcelain paste using a large CelStick and leaving a thick ridge down the centre (use a grooved board if you wish). Rub a small amount of cold cream onto the edges of the large gladioli petal shape. Place the rolled-out paste on top of the petal shape, making sure that the thick ridge is central. Roll over the top of the paste against the cutting sheet using a small rolling pin. Remove the excess paste and then gently remove the tepal shape from the cutting sheet.

2. Insert a moistened 24 gauge white wire into at least half the length of the thick ridge of the tepal. Dust the surface of the paste with a small amount of cornflour and then place the tepal onto the orchid veiner, pressing it firmly with the side of your hand to give maximum veining. Turn the tepal over and vein the other side. Remove from the veiner and place the tepal back onto the board. Frill the edge using the ceramic silk veining tool. Some irises have more frilling than others; with most flowers I tend not to frill too much, but in the case of the bearded iris I feel it looks more attractive with quite a lot of frills. Pinch a ridge down the centre of the tepal on the upper surface. Allow to dry over the edge of a large piece of foam to create the characteristic curl that the 'falls' have. Repeat to make three tepals. Allow to dry slightly.

The Beard

The beard is a raised furry platform that is attached to each of the 'fall' tepals. They are used as an aid to help direct insects to the pollen hidden at the base of the petal. There are several methods that can be used to create the beard (some people represent them with a pipe cleaner- very bizarre!), but I prefer the following. Roll out a small piece of white paste and cut out a rectangular shape using a sharp scalpel (you might find that the blade cuts easier if you apply a small amount of cold cream to the blade - be very careful not to cut yourself). Next make lots of tiny cuts into the edges of both of the long sides of the shape (it should look like a comb on each side). Carefully remove the shape from the board and fold down the centre, so that the tips of each of the cuts are in line with one another. Next fold the length of the shape into a very relaxed concertina shape to form a bushy beard (you should not need to use glue or moisture at this stage). Place the beard on its side onto the board and trim off some of the depth from the base using a scalpel. Repeat to make three beards.

Apply a line of glue to the centre of each of the tepals and attach a beard to each one. Trim off any excess. Allow to dry.

Style Crest

1. This is the forked petal that is attached to the falls above the beard. Roll out some white paste leaving a thick ridge down the centre. Apply some cold cream to the crest shape on the cutting sheet and then cut out as for the tepals. Insert a moistened 26 gauge white wire into at least half the length of the thick ridge, holding the petal firmly between your finger and thumb to prevent the wire from escaping.

2. Place the petal on the board and work the two pointed parts of the crest with the broad end of the dresden tool, to create a double frilled effect. You will need to use quite deep smooth strokes against the paste onto the board to give a veined as well as a frilled appearance to the petal. Pinch the upper surface of the petal firmly between your finger and thumb to create a ridge down the whole length of the petal. Place the petal onto a pad and then cup the two pointed sections back using a small ball tool and a rolling action. Curve the length of the crest petal gently and allow to firm up a little. Repeat to make three crest petals.

Standard Tepals

These upright tepals are made in the same way as the fall tepals, but the pinched ridge should be much more subtle. Allow to dry with a gentle curve.

Colouring

Dust the beard on each tepal with a mixture of Daffodil and Sunflower sugarcraft dust - be careful not to get too much yellow onto the surface of the tepal, especially if you are planning to use purple dust for the main colour of the flower as the finished result can look a little murky. The dark flower pictured was dusted with purple craft dust with a touch of Deep Magenta added. The paler flower was dusted with a mixture of Edelweiss and Lavender sugarcraft dust. Dust the large tepals from the edges towards the beard using a flat dusting brush. Dust the style crest petals from the base towards the forked end, leaving them paler towards the tips.

Assembly

1. Tape together a crest petal and a fall tepal using half-width Nile Green floristry tape. Adjust the crest petal so that it sits neatly over the beard. Repeat with the remaining fall tepals and crest petals.

2. Tape together the three standard tepals onto the end of an 18 gauge wire, again using half-width Nile Green floristry tape. Adjust the position of the standards, if required - remember that they should all curl inwards. Next position and tape in each of the crest and fall tepals - they should sit in between each of the

standards. It is at this stage that you might need to add a greater depth of colour to achieve a more balanced and pleasing result. If the tepals are still damp then you have the ideal opportunity to re-shape them. If they have dried and you would like to re-shape them, simply hold the flower over the steam from a kettle; this will soften them and allow you to adjust them a little.

Buds

1. Tape over a half length of 20 or 22 gauge wire with half-width Nile Green tape. Bend a large open hook in the end of the wire. Roll a ball of white paste into a cone shape. apply some glue to the hooked wire and insert it into the base of the cone. Neaten the base by simply pinching the paste onto the wire.

2. Tape together three pieces of 24 gauge wire at one end. Open up the wire to form a cage. Rub a small amount of cold cream onto each of the wires. Insert the bud, tip first into the cage. Pull each of the wires tight into the paste to make three deep indents. Pinch out the paste from in between each of the wires to form three petals. Remove the cage. Twist the three petals around to form a neat bud shape. Neaten up the base if required.

Ovary

Attach a ball of Sap Green paste at the base of the bud and the flower. Pinch the ball tightly where it meets the base of the bud and flower. Divide the surface into three subtle sections using a scalpel. Dust with Vine green sugarcraft dust.

Bracts

There are two bracts to each flower and bud and you will need to alter the size accordingly. Roll out some very pale Sap Green paste. Cut out two bract shapes, either using the shapes provided on the cutting sheet or simply by cutting them out free-hand using a sharp scalpel. Vein the surface using either a dried sweetcorn husk or the Asi-es No. 22 veiner. Place the bract shapes onto a pad and soften the edges using a medium ball tool and a rolling action, working half on the paste and half on the pad. Pinch each bract on the veined side between your finger and thumb to form a central ridge. Moisten

each bract slightly with some diluted glue and attach the bracts, overlapping one over the other on top of the ovary. Dust with cream-coloured sugarcraft dust and then some Vine green.

Assembly

1. Tape an iris flower-head onto two lengths of 18 gauge wire using half-width Nile Green floristry tape. A little down the stem add a bud and then perhaps add another one further down the stem, or tape two flowers together onto one stem.

2. Next add two larger bracts at each of the junctions on the stem. Dust as for the smaller bracts. Dust the main stem to a dark green. Allow to dry. Spray the whole flower stem with a matt spray varnish.

Leaves

1. The leaves are very long and are quite awkward to make in cold porcelain; however they do enhance the finished arrangement of irises, so you will need to persevere! Roll out a long strip of Sap Green-coloured cold porcelain (not too thinly). Grease the leaf shape on the cutting sheet and place the paste on top. Roll over the surface with a rolling pin to cut out the shape, and remove the excess paste and leaf from the cutting sheet. Vein the surface of the paste on both sides using either a dried piece of sweetcorn husk, the Asi-es No. 22 veiner or the length of a packet of 26 gauge wire.

2. Tape over a length of 22 or 20 gauge wire with half-width Nile Green floristry tape. Apply some glue to approximately $3^1/_2$ - 4 inches of the wire. Place the wire on top of the leaf and press into the surface of the paste. Pick up the leaf and the wire, and quickly pinch the paste from the back of the leaf firmly onto the wire. Pinch the whole leaf from the base to the tip to give it more shape. Bend the leaf as required. Allow to firm up, but not to dry, before dusting.

3. Dust with Holly/Ivy and Vine sugarcraft dust and then overdust with some Sap Green craft dust. Allow to dry and then spray with a satin varnish in a well-ventilated area.

Monkshood
(Aconitum cammarum)

*M*onkshood is available as a cut flower for most of the year, but as a garden plant it flowers from late summer through to early autumn. The whole plant is very poisonous - but you could also say deadly attractive! The stems are very useful for adding height, as well as plenty of interest to arrangements. Monkshood varieties include the colours of white, white tinged with purple, purple and dark blue.

AD

Materials

Cold porcelain: ivory and Sap Green

Craft dust: purple, Sap Green and dark green (a blend of Sap Green, Jade, Burnt Sienna and black)

Sugarcraft dust: Holly/Ivy

33, 26, 24 and 20 gauge white wire

Small white seed-head stamens

Nile Green floristry tape

Anita's Satin découpage varnish diluted with an equal amount of water

Hi-tack glue or glue gun and glue sticks

Equipment

Monkshood flower and leaf templates page 37

Stamens

1. Glue a small group of small seed-head stamens onto the end of a 24 gauge wire using either the Hi-tack glue or glue gun. Allow the glue to set before colouring the stamens. Dust the tips with a mixture of purple craft dust and black sugarcraft dust. In the real flower there are two very long nectaries that are hidden underneath the hood of the flower - you do not need to worry about adding these for general display work. However if you are planning to enter a specimen class in a cold porcelain exhibition then you will need to add them. If you are working to a specimen class standard then it is advisable to have a fresh sample of monkshood to copy. The nectaries are complicated and can be only made accurately if you are copying directly from the fresh flower.

Side Tepals (The Arms)

1. Trace the tepal shapes from the templates on page 37 and transfer the shapes onto some thin plastic. Cut out the shapes using a small pair of scissors. It is much easier to make this flower with individually wired tepals. Roll out a small amount of ivory paste leaving a fine thick ridge down the centre. Use the side tepal template and a sharp scalpel to cut out the shape.

2. Insert a moistened 33 gauge white wire into the thick ridge and pinch the paste firmly onto the wire. Place the tepal onto a pad and soften the edges with a medium ball tool. Cup the centre with the ball tool using a rolling action. Pick up the petal and curl back one edge using your fingers. Repeat to make two side petals.

Base Tepals (The Legs)

1. Roll out some more ivory-coloured paste and cut out the leg tepals as described for the arm tepals. Insert a moistened 33 gauge white wire into each tepal and again pinch the paste firmly onto the wire to make them secure. Soften the edges, but be careful not to frill the paste. Draw down a central vein on each tepal using the fine end of the dresden veining tool.

2. Tape the two side tepals onto the base of the stamens using quarter-width Nile Green floristry tape. Trim off the excess wire to avoid a bulky stem. Tape the legs onto the flower next. The flower is easier to make if the paste is still damp at this stage as it enables you to manipulate the shaping more easily. Curl the base petals down slightly.

The Hood

1. Roll out some ivory-coloured paste and cut out the hood using the required template and scalpel. Place the paste onto a pad and soften the edges. Draw down a strong vein to divide the two sides of the hood and then hollow out the two sides using a small ball tool.

2. Dilute some Hi-tack glue with a small amount of water and then

paint a fine line of glue onto the back edge of the tepal. Pick up the tepal and carefully join the two edges together. Trim off any excess or uneven edges with a pair of fine scissors. Leave the very base of the hood open slightly so that it sits easily over the other tepals.

3. Apply a small amount of glue at the base of the side tepals and then position the hood over the top. Neaten the base of the hood tepal against the side tepals. Allow to dry slightly before colouring. You will need to make several flowers to complete one stem of monkshood.

Colouring

Dust each flower with your chosen shade of blue or purple - the flowers illustrated have been dusted with purple craft dust.

Buds

1. You will need to make lots of buds to complete a stem of monkshood. Cut several short lengths of 26 gauge wire. Tape over the length of each and then bend a small hook on the end.

2. Attach a ball of paste onto the end of a hooked wire. Flatten the sides of the ball and then pinch a ridge down the centre, to represent the shape of the hood. You will need to graduate the size of the buds. Dust as for the flower, introducing some green dust to smaller buds.

Bracts

Each flower and bud has a bract at the base of its stem. These are very simple to make, but as you need a lot they can be time-consuming. Blend a piece of green paste onto a fine wire and then smooth the paste between your palms. Place the slender shape onto the board and then flatten using the flat side of a rubber veiner. If the shape looks uneven, you will need to trim it with scissors. Draw down a central vein. Dust with Holly/Ivy sugarcraft dust.

Leaves

Make some templates as before using the leaf template shapes on page 37. Roll out some Sap Green paste leaving a thick ridge down the centre. Cut out a leaf shape using a template and scalpel. Soften the edges and then draw down a central vein and a side vein on each section. You will need to make one of each shape to make up a complete leaf. Dust with Holly/Ivy, dark green and then tinge the edges with some purple. Dip into a half découpage glaze (see equipment list).

Assembly

1. Start the stem by taping a small bud and bract onto a 20 gauge wire using half-width Nile Green floristry tape. Continue to add buds and bracts graduating in size down the stem. When you have created a reasonable length, start to introduce the flower-heads, again with a bract and leaving a length of each flower stem on show.

2. Tape the leaves onto the stem alternating them from side to side down the stem. Dust the main stem with a light covering of the two greens used on the leaves. Bend the whole stem into an attractive shape.

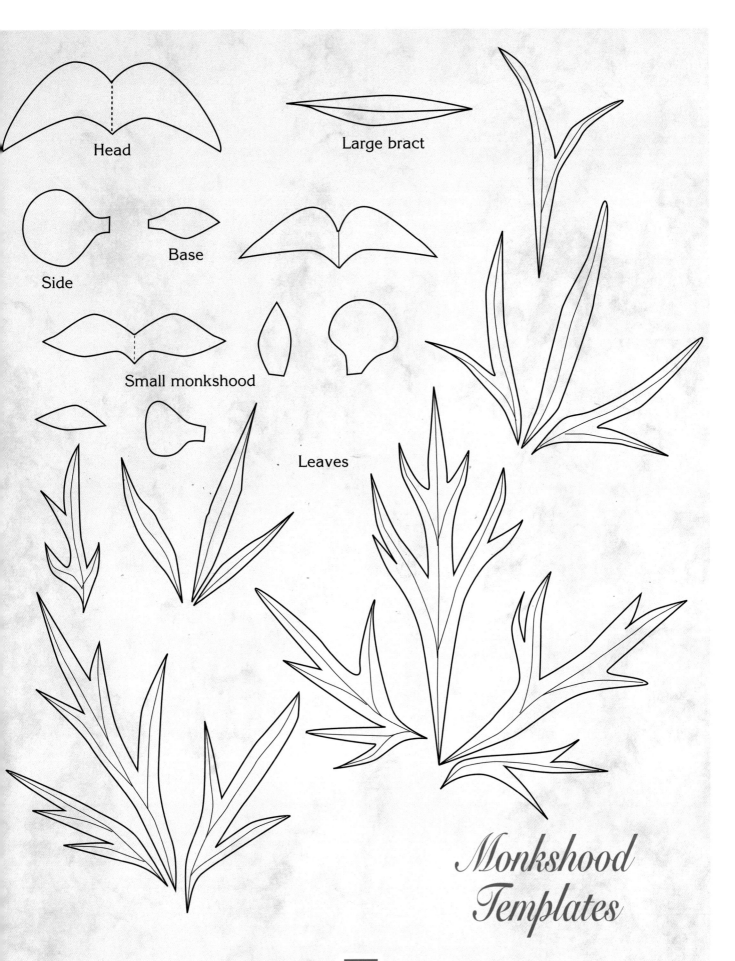

Head

Large bract

Side

Base

Small monkshood

Leaves

Monkshood
Templates

37

Japanese Anemone
(Anemone hupehensis, var. Japonica)

The original colour of this beautiful flower was pink, but in cultivation there are plants that produce dark pink, lilac, dark red and white flowers in single, semi-double and double forms. In fact the original was not Japanese at all, but Chinese! It is however the Japanese that we have to thank for this hybrid form. Perhaps it would be easier to use its other common name which is the windflower. This attractive plant flowers from late summer through to the autumn months, providing a much needed splash of colour at that time of year.

AD

Materials

Cold porcelain: white and mid-Sap Green

Gouache: yellow and Permanent White

Craft dust: yellow, Deep Magenta and dark green (a blend of Sap Green, Jade, Burnt Sienna and black)

Sugarcraft dust: Holly/Ivy, Edelweiss, Thrift, Cyclamen and Daffodil

28, 26 and 24 gauge white wire

20 and 18 gauge wire

White seed-head stamens

Nile Green floristry tape

Impex glue

Anita's Satin découpage varnish (diluted with an equal amount of water) or satin spray varnish

Matt spray varnish

Equipment

Tinkertech Two Simple Leaf cutters or Australian Rose Petal cutter set

Great Impressions Christmas Rose veiner (round and cupped)

Asi-es Large Leaf veiner No. 27

Japanese anemone leaf templates page 41

Ovary

Tape over a length of 20 gauge wire with half-width Nile Green floristry tape. Bend an open hook in the end of the wire using pliers. Roll a ball of Sap Green paste and attach to the hooked end of the wire using a small amount of glue. Neaten the base of the ovary and then texture the surface using the point of a sharp scalpel. Allow to dry. Dust very gently with a mixture of Daffodil and Holly/Ivy sugarcraft dust.

Stamens

1. Pick up a small group of seed-head stamens. Pull them into line so that their heads are at an even height. Apply some glue to the stamens, starting from the centre and then blending the glue into the length of the stamens leaving a short length free from glue at their ends. Repeat until you formed several stamen groups. Allow to dry slightly, but not completely. Trim the stamens at both ends of the groups to leave two short lengths. Apply some more glue to the base of each set and then attach to the base of the ovary. Repeat this with several more sets of stamens, until you have formed a neat ring of stamens around the ovary. Allow to dry.

2. Paint the very tips of the stamens with yellow gouache, diluted with a small amount of water. Allow to dry and then dust a small amount of yellow craft dust over the top of the painted tips.

Tepals

1. Add a minute amount of Permanent White gouache to the cold porcelain. Roll out some paste thinly onto a grooved board using a rolling pin. Cut out six tepals using either the largest leaf cutter or the Australian rose petal cutter, or a combination of the two (this will depend upon the effect you want to create). Some plants produce double flowers and some produce flowers with only five tepals so it is basically left to your own taste.

2. Cut lengths of 28 gauge white wire into four pieces, moisten the ends of the wires and insert one into the thick ridge of each petal (into the pointed end).

3. Vein each tepal using the double-sided Christmas rose veiner, pressing firmly to give strong veining. You might find that you will need to dust the mould or the paste before you vein to prevent the paste sticking to the mould.

4. Place the tepals onto a pad and soften the edges using a medium ball tool, working half on the paste and half on the pad (do not frill the edges - this is not a frilly flower). Cup the centre of each tepal gently. Some varieties of Japanese anemone have three smaller tepals on the back of the flower. To make these use a smaller cutter from one of the petal sets and make in the same way as the larger tepals. Allow the tepals to firm up a little before constructing the flower; they are much easier to dust once the flower has been assembled.

Assembly and Colouring

1. First tape three tepals around the set of stamens using half-width Nile Green floristry tape. Tape another three tepals onto the stem, positioning them in between the previous three. If you have made the three smaller tepals add these next, positioning each over a join in the second layer.

2. Mix some Deep Magenta craft dust with some Edelweiss sugarcraft dust. Dust each of the tepals gently with a

flat brush and some of the dust mixture, starting with the edges and then applying a small amount at the base of each tepal on the back and front. The outer three tepals should have some stronger colour on their backs, so increase the magenta colour and then add some Thrift or Cyclamen dust in a strong line.

Leaves

1. Trace the templates on page 41 and transfer the design onto some card or preferably some thin plastic (from an ice cream container, margarine tub or model shop). Cut out the designs using a small pair of sharp scissors.

2. Roll out some Sap Green paste leaving a thick ridge down the centre. Place one of the templates on top of the paste and cut around the shape using a sharp scalpel.

3. Insert a moistened wire into at least half the length of the leaf (the gauge of the wire will depend upon the size of the leaf - the larger leaves will need a 24 gauge wire). Flatten and thin out the edges of the leaf using the broad end of the dresden tool, to give more interest and serration to the edges of the leaf. Dust the surface of the leaf and then vein using the Asi-es leaf veiner, using the side of your hand to press the leaf onto the veiner. Remove from the veiner and place the leaf onto a pad. Soften the edges, working half on the paste and half on the pad using the medium metal ball tool.

Pinch the leaf from the back to emphasise the central vein. Allow to slightly dry slightly before dusting.

4. Dust the edges of the leaves with a mixture of Thrift and Cyclamen sugarcraft dust with a small amount of Deep Magenta craft dust added. Next colour the leaves with a good layer of Holly/Ivy sugarcraft dust, working from the base of each leaf towards the edges. Overdust with a layer of darker green to add more depth to the leaves. Allow to dry.

5. Dilute some satin découpage varnish with an equal amount of water and then dip each leaf into the milky solution. Shake off the excess and if there are any air bubbles of the surface blow them off. The leaf should dry quite quickly and the glaze will leave a partial shine on the leaves.

6. Tape the leaves together into their groups of three using half-width Nile Green tape.

Buds

1. Tape over a half length of 24 gauge wire with half-width tape. Bend a small open hook in the end of the wire using pliers. Roll a ball of pale Sap Green paste, moisten the hook on the wire and insert it into the ball. Neaten the join between the wire and the ball. Roll the tip of the bud into a slight point. Divide the surface of the bud into three sections using a sharp scalpel. Using a finer touch with the

scalpel, mark several striations on the buds surface. Repeat to make buds of various sizes.

2. To make a larger bud, use a larger ball of white paste and repeat the method described above. Allow to dry.

3. Roll three small balls of green paste in turn, into three teardrop shapes. Flatten each with the flat side of a rubber veiner to form three sepal shapes. Place each on the palm of your hand and cup slightly using a small ball tool. Moisten each tepal and attach to the bud. You should be able to still see some of the white paste showing through.

4. Dust all of the buds and their stems lightly with Holly/Ivy sugarcraft dust. Catch the tips of the buds with some Cyclamen/Thrift/Deep Magenta mix.

Assembly

Tape the buds together with their heads at different levels onto an 18 gauge wire. Add a flower, leaving a fairly long stem on show. At the junction between all of the buds and flowers you will need to add two sets of the smaller leaf triplets, leaving very little stem on show. Form another flower/bud/leaf group and then tape the two groups together, adding another two sets of slightly larger leaves where the two groups join the main stem. Add more 18 gauge wire to lengthen and strengthen the stem. Add some larger leaves to complete the stem. Dust the stems with some Holly/Ivy sugarcraft dust. Bend the buds and flowers a little to make a more attractive display.

Japanese Anemone Leaf Templates

Callicarpa Berries
(Callicarpa bodinieri giraldii)

Callicarpa is a shrub that originates from China. It produces clusters of lilac flowers followed in the autumn by small, glossy lilac-purple berries that have an almost metallic surface. They are very attractive if combined with other autumnal flowers and foliage, adding instant interest to an arrangement and they would also look very pretty and unusual in an autumnal bridal bouquet.

AD

Materials

Cold porcelain coloured with Brilliant Violet and Permanent White gouache

Craft dust: purple, Deep Magenta and Burnt Sienna

Sugarcraft dust: black, Edelweiss, Tinsel Town Amethyst and Metallic Lustre Snowflake

36 gauge silk-covered wire (available from 'The Scientific Wire Company')

20 gauge wire

Brown floristry tape

Gloss and matt spray varnish

Berries

1. Cut several short lengths of 36 gauge silk-covered wire. Bend a tiny hook in the end of each length. Add some Permanent White and Brilliant Violet gouache to the paste. Try not to make the base colour too dark as this will produce too heavy a finish - it is better to start paler and add depth with dust afterwards.

2. Roll lots of small balls of paste. Moisten the hook on each wire in turn, and then insert each one into a ball. Neaten the area where the paste joins the wire and try to make the berries evenly round. You will need to make approximately 80 - 100 berries for each stem. Allow to firm up a little before dusting and assembling the stem.

Colouring and Assembly

1. It is easier to dust the berries after they have been wired together and taped onto the twig. First of all tape the berries together into small groups of three to five using quarter width Nile Green floristry tape. To form the twig, start by taping over a 20 gauge wire with half-width brown floristry tape. Next tape in several groups of berries to form a cluster at the top of the twig. Leave a gap on the twig and then tape in another cluster. Repeat this as many times as necessary until you have created the length of stem you require. As you work down the twig you must remember to make the thickness fairly even. To do this you can either tape over several times with half-width tape, or you can shred some kitchen paper into thin strips and wrap them around the twig, and then tape over the top. To make larger twigs you will need to join several shorter twigs to the main twig.

2. Dust the berries gently with layers of Deep Magenta and purple craft dust with a touch of Edelweiss sugarcraft dust added. The berries have a slight metallic finish and to create this, dust them with a tiny amount of Snowflake dust and then a touch of Amethyst dust. You might need to increase the purple colouring to concentrate the colour a little more, but be very careful not to over do it. Spray the berries with the gloss spray paint or paint them with a layer of gloss découpage varnish (whichever method you decide to use, be very careful not to glaze the twig itself. You might prefer to colour and glaze the berries before you assemble the twig - but this can be time consuming and equally as fiddly. Bend the twig a little to make a more interesting piece and then spray with a matt varnish.

Autumn Arrangement

*T*his beautiful arrangement
includes several of the more
unusual autumn flowers, fruit
and foliage. It was only on
completion of this piece that
I realised that each of the
subjects originated from
China.

AD

Flowers

3 stems of callicarpa berries

4 stems of monkshood

7 Japanese anemones with buds and leaves

Several pieces of assorted foliage

Equipment

18 gauge wire

Nile Green floristry tape

Pliers

Wire cutters

Green florists' Staysoft or artists' Plasticine

Green glass dish

Large round metallic plate

Glue gun and glue sticks

Preparation

1. If any of the flower stems are on the weak side you will need to strengthen them by taping an 18 gauge wire onto the main stem using half-width floristry tape.

2. Glue a large clump of Staysoft into the glass dish using the glue sticks and glue gun. Place the glass dish on top of the metallic plate.

Assembly

1. Bend a hook in the end of each of the anemone stems as required (this will hold the stems in position better than if they simply had straight ends). Start by arranging the taller stems of Japanese anemone into the Staysoft. Gradually add the remaining flowers, staggering them to create an attractive balanced design.

2. Next add the three stems of callicarpa berries to create more shape to the arrangement.

3. Finally add the monkshood to give more height and also depth with the shorter stems. The back and base of the arrangement also might need more depth which can be achieved by using any other pieces of Japanese anemone and monkshood leaves that you may have. Disguise the back of the Staysoft with extra pieces of foliage.

Specimen Rose

*T*his rose is in much demand. I am asked to demonstrate this more often than any other flower in my repertoire. Its a good thing I never get tired of making them! I seldom have a sample as people who know me well manage to wheedle them out of me as keepsakes. Flattering I know, but I sometimes wish I could learn to say NO! The rose is made with twenty petals, ten forming the half rose, and ten wired petals.

TP

Materials

Cold porcelain with Permanent White and a little Primary Yellow gouache added to make it just off-white

Craft dust: yellow, Scarlet, Sap Green and Deep Magenta

Sugarcraft dust: Alabaster Bridal Satin, Edelweiss and Vine

Oil paints: Sap Green and Terre Verte

Thinners with paint drying liquid added

20 and 14 gauge green wires

28, 26 and 24 gauge white wires

Nile Green floristry tape

1/2 " and 1" polystyrene balls

Diluted Anita's Satin découpage varnish

Equipment

Set of large Tinkertech Two Rose Petal cutters and the largest cutter from the set of 5 smaller cutters

Jem Lines Black Rose Leaf cutters and the large Green Rose Leaf cutter

Great Impressions very large Rose Petal veiner

Great Impressions large Briar Rose Leaf veiner

Orchard Products Calyx cutter No. R11B

Apple tray cups (preferably smaller, cardboard ones, cut into individual cups)

Method

1. Hook a 14 gauge wire and moisten with glue. Pull through a 1" styrofoam ball until it is firmly imbedded. Squash the part of the ball above the wire into a point. Moisten with glue. Take a chunk of paste, roll it into a ball and squash it into a flat circle. Insert the wire through the centre. Gather the paste around the ball, pulling the excess upwards to form a cone. Repeat this process with smaller styrofoam balls to make the buds. The styrofoam balls are used for their lightness, and because they cost less than the equivalent amount of paste you would need to create the cones. For a very small bud just use paste to form the cone. The cones for the buds can be on 20 gauge wires. Allow all the cones to dry properly.

2. Tape the wires with Nile Green tape.

3. Roll out the paste fairly thinly. Cut seven petals with the smallest of the three large rose petal cutters. You must ensure that the petals are larger than the cones they are to cover. Place them under a plastic mat to keep them from drying out.

4. Layer One: Place a petal on a Billy's block and soften the edge with the ball tool. Cover the petal with glue and attach to the cone, ensuring that the petal is higher than the tip of the cone and you have a very tight centre. The cone must be completely concealed.

5. Layer Two: Remove three petals from under the mat. Place them on the foam pad and soften the edges. Dust the petal veiners with cornflour and vein all three petals. With the pointed ends of the petals towards you, apply glue to the left hand side of each of the petals. Place the cone and first layer onto the petal, making sure the petal is higher than the previous layer. The join of the petal already on the cone must be to the centre of this first petal. Fasten down the glued edge of the petal. Place the next glued edge of a petal to the right of the one already stuck on the cone and slip the third petal to the right of the second petal, tucking it beneath the first petal. Pull down on the edge of the petals to ensure a tight centre, but at the same time ensure that the petals are taller than the first layer. Glue these petals in place, furling the outer edges very slightly.

6. Layer Three: Repeat as for the previous layer, but the glued edges of these three petals are tucked under the furled edges of the previous layer. Once again see that these petals are higher than the previous layer and furl back the edges more than the previous layer.

7. Layer Four: Roll out fresh paste and cut three petals using the largest cutter. Soften the edges on the foam pad, Dust the veiners with cornflour and vein the petals. Using your thumbs and forefingers gently cup the petals without removing the veining. Put the glue on these petals in a 'V' at the pointed base of the petals. The furled edges of the previous layer go to the centre of each of these petals, each petal is spiralled underneath the previous one. Make sure that the petals are taller than the previous layer, but not by a great deal. This layer of petals neatens the whole cone. If the paste is too long against the wire cut off the excess. Furl the edges of the petals to attractive shapes using the CelSticks. Remember not to curl the petals too much or you could get an ugly looking petal after the shrinkage.

8. Layer Five: Cut out five petals with the largest cutter. The paste should be thicker at the pointed end. Cut three 24 gauge wires into thirds. Hook one end. Moisten the end of the wire with glue and slide it into the thickened paste at the point of the petal. Soften the edge of the petal on the foam pad. Dust the veiner, vein the petal. Lift the edge of the petal onto the forefinger of your left hand and using a medium frilling stick or a Holly Products ceramic silk veining tool veining tool gently frill the edge of the petal. Curl the edges of the petals with a CelStick and arrange the curled edge over the edge of the apple cup. Repeat this process for all five petals.

9. Layer Six: This layer is a repeat of the previous layer. Make sure that each petal is cupped and the curling of the edge of each petal is different. Set the petals aside to dry.

Buds

1. The buds are made the same as the flowers, just stopping the process at earlier layers. It is sensible to have more buds and half roses (this is the layer before the wired petals) than full roses.

2. Make a Mexican hat. Roll out the paste with a CelStick making sure you have a 90 degree angle between the pedicel and the sepals. Place the cutter over the Mexican hat. Cut it out. Elongate each sepal. Place the calyx on the foam pad and cup each sepal using your small ball tool. Use the fine curved scissors to cut the hairy bits at the edge

of the sepals. Two sepals do not have any cuts at all. These are the sepals that are attached to the bud, over the joins between petals before gradually sticking the other sepals in place. Dust the inside of the calyx with Alabaster sugarcraft dust.

3. Run a cocktail stick around the base of the rose to create the indentation above the ovary. Fasten the ovary tightly to the wire. Arrange the sepals attractively.

Leaves

1. You have to decide on the style of your leaflets. A specimen rose can be a hybrid. The new hybrid roses tend to have much larger leaves than the older roses. They also quite often have compound leaves with only three leaflets instead of the five used in the past. If you decide you want to use only one size of cutter go for the large green leaf cutter, otherwise you can mix and match that cutter with the black ones creating a compound leaf made up of five leaflets. This is a single large leaf which can then have four similar sized leaves below it, or two sets of two leaves in decreasing sizes. You need a minimum of fifteen leaves for each bud, half rose and rose.

2. It is quicker to make these leaves rolling them flat and folding the leaf around the wire as described earlier in the book. Soften the edges of the leaves before veining them. Arrange the leaves into some interesting shapes, but by and large they are fairly flat.

3. Paint the leaves with varying amounts of Sap Green and Terre Verte to get some variation into the greenery. Remember the underside of the leaves are paler than the upper surfaces.

4. Dust the edges of the leaves with Scarlet craft dust and then dust over the leaves with Sap Green craft dust. When the leaves are dry dip them into diluted Anita's varnish. Allow to dry.

5. Tape the leaflets into the chosen compound leaves and set aside.

First Stage of Assembling the Full Rose

Using half-width tape bind the wired petals behind the half rose. Keep tugging at the wires to bed the petals in firmly so no wires are visible. A better look is obtained if two or three petals are pulled between petals that are already fastened in place.

Dusting the Rose

If you prefer you can dust the petals of the rose before you put them together. This gives a much too 'neat' appearance. Dusting the rose after it is assembled breathes life into the flower.

1. Dust the back of the petals with yellow craft dust mixed with white sugarcraft dust. Dust a little yellow and Vine at the base of the back and front of each wired petal and using a fine brush dust into the rose with these colours as well.

2. Mix the colour for the petals. Load your brush and tap off the excess dust onto a piece of kitchen paper. Tightly hold the rose, upright and firmly tap the colour into the centre of the rose three times. Now concentrate on the front of the petals. Dust the colour from the edge inwards, turning the rose in your left hand. When the front of all the petals have been dusted repeat the process on the back of each petal, leaving more of the petal yellow. To highlight the veins very carefully and gently brush across them. A tiny amount of colour will be caught on the veins, high-lighting them.

3. When all the petals are dusted make the calyx as described for the bud, dusting the inside with Alabaster sugarcraft dust. The sepals are, on the full rose, left hanging down after the indentation above the ovary has been made. Before the sepals become dry dust the outside of the sepals with a green suited to the colour of the flower.

4. Spray the rose with matt varnish.

Final Assembly

Tape groups of leaves onto half length 20 gauge wires. Tape other groups onto the stems of the buds, half roses and full rose. To achieve the very best results it is helpful to have a real rose on hand to look at the precise positioning of the various elements. An attractive result can be achieved if a group of leaves is fastened onto the stem so that the leaves are positioned above the rose. The buds very often look better if they are arranged slightly lower than the full rose. When all elements have been taped together, cut out the wire that is not required, dust the stem attractively and then paint PVA glue over the stem.

Miniatures

Miniatures

*M*iniature modelling requires a whole new set of skills and a completely different approach to modelling flowers. Gone is the precision, in its place is the overall impression. This sounds contradictory, but if you try too hard to make a miniature look real it tends to become stiff and unattractive. I actually work in two distinct sizes. One for dolls' houses and one for eggs. The rose spray was intended for an egg, the rest for a dolls' house.

I find very few cutters are needed when making miniatures. Most of it is done almost free-hand. The things you need most are good eyesight, a lot of time and patience (I possess none of these!). I became interested in working in miniatures when at a sugarcraft exhibition I overheard someone say 'Of course, Tombi just can't make small flowers'. I was always keen on a dare!

Since I started making miniature flowers and arrangements to the scale of an inch to a foot which is standard for dolls' houses, I have become fascinated by the whole concept. I have a lovely dolls' house my Uncle Charles made for me for Christmas when I was six. My granddaughter adores it. I'd love to get one just as an ongoing project, but there is just nowhere to put it in my house. The best pots for miniatures are made by Carol Mann. She specialises in tiny pottery, and each piece is exquisite on its own. It is best to attend an exhibition and buy them from her there. Not many dolls' house shops actually stock her pots.

TP

Equipment Required to make Miniature Flowers

Sets of tiny Kemper cutters (4 in a set, 2 sizes)

Miniature and Micro cutters (available from CelCrafts)

Tiny metal ball tools (available from CelCrafts)

A range of miniature cutters made by Fine Cut Cutters of Australia (available from Pat-a-Cake, Birmingham)

Angela Priddy miniature cutters

Orchard Products cutters Nos. F10, D2, N7, N8, DY7, DY8, MF1, R15 and R16

36 gauge silk-covered wire (available from 'The Scientific Wire Company')

32, 30 and 28 gauge wires

Floristry tape

Glue and applicator

Suitable pots

Florists' Staysoft

Model railway gravel

Floristry tape in different colours

Foam pad

Assorted gouache and oil paints

Assorted craft and sugarcraft dusts

Silk and matt spray varnish

Bonsai

Requirements

Cold porcelain

36 gauge silk-covered wire (available from 'The Scientific Wire Company')

Smallest Kemper Blossom cutter

Metal ball tools

The cherry blossom bonsai was created by making very small balls of pink paste on 36 gauge scientific wire. Tiny pieces of green were added for calyxes. The more open flowers were shaped around tinier balls and the cutter used was the smallest blossom plunger cutter made by Kemper. The outer petals were slightly cupped with a range of very small ball tools on a foam pad. Do this very gently or you will ruin

many a blossom. The leaves were made by the 'splat' method. Take a tiny piece of green paste, form a tiny cone shape, add glue to a small piece of 36 gauge wire, stick it into the paste, place on your non-stick board and flatten ('splat') with a palette knife or something similar. Gently pinch the leaf to give it some character and movement.

Gradually tape the component pieces together using quarter-width tape and then when you get to the trunk, half-width tape. When the trunk is long enough, separate the remaining wires into three and tape them to form the roots. Place a small piece of Staysoft in the chosen dish. Bend the tree to shape over the Staysoft, add more Staysoft to secure, make the final adjustments to the arrangement, add a little glue to the surface of the Staysoft and cover with gravel. With small brushes add judicious dusting.

Miniature Rose
(for egg)

Requirements

Cold porcelain

Sugarcraft dust: Alabaster

30 and 28 gauge wires

Orchard Products cutters Nos. F10, R15 and R16

Great Impressions smallest Curiosity Rose veiner

Make tiny cones on 28 gauge wires. The cone must fit easily inside one petal of the F10 cutter. Allow to dry. Roll out paste very thinly, cut out one or two layers of petals depending on the size of your rose. Three layers becomes unwieldy. Smaller buds can be made by dissecting a blossom shape into two, then making a bud with two petals and another with three.

Soften the edges of the petals on your foam pad with a ball tool. Moisten with a little glue. Attach one petal and spiral it

around the cone, miss a petal and attach it and the one opposite it around the first petal, then bring up the two final petals and add them to the flower. If you want this to be a rose add a calyx with a tiny ovary. Dust the inside of the calyx with the Alabaster sugarcraft dust and use a green

to suit the rose for colouring the calyx. If you want to add a second layer of petals do so. Soften the edges, and cup the centres of the petals and stick the petals over joins from previous layers. Once again add a calyx. Dust the roses when they are completed.

Caladium

Requirements

Cold porcelain

30 gauge wire

Orchard Products Maidenhair Fern cutter No. MF1

Cut out the leaves, choosing the shapes that suit the plant most. Soften the edges of the leaves with a ball tool on the foam pad. Bend a 30 gauge wire at right angles, moisten it with glue and press the wire against the leaf, with the wire emerging from behind the broadest part of the leaf. Set aside to dry and then decorate using a very fine brush and diluted pink and green gouache. Fill a suitable pot with Staysoft, cover with glue and then modelling gravel and using fine nosed pliers or tweezers push the wires into the Staysoft. Very gently colour the wires with diluted green colouring when they are in place.

When the decoration has dried spray with matt varnish.

Mother in Law's Tongue

Requirements

Cold porcelain

28 gauge wire

Roll pieces of paste onto 28 gauge wires and use the 'splat' method. If the leaves are not quite right trim them with a pair of fine scissors. Twist and curl the leaves gently. Have a picture of a real plant next to you when you decorate it. The leaves were dusted green before painting in the yellow edge with oil paint. I used Burnt Sienna oil paint and a little thinner to paint on the striking markings. Once the leaves are dry glaze them with découpage varnish. Fill a suitable pot with Staysoft, cover with modelling sand and with fine nosed pliers or tweezers push the wire into the Staysoft. Don't have the wires too short, it gives better support if the wires in the Staysoft are longer rather than shorter.

Daffodils and Tulips

Requirements

Cold Porcelain coloured green, yellow and pink

28 gauge wire

Miniature or Micro Iris Centre cutters for the tulip (available from CelCrafts)

Orchard Products cutter No. N7 for the Daffodil

Daffodil

Make a tiny hook on a 28 gauge wire. Put a minute piece of green paste over this. Make sure it is extremely small. Set aside to dry. Take a teardrop shape of yellow paste. Open the broad end with a cocktail stick and frill the edge on your forefinger. Moisten the dried piece of green paste with glue and pull into the centre of the frilled centre. Arrange the frill to your satisfaction. Set aside to dry. Cut out several shapes with the N7 cutter and put them under a plastic mat. You will waste a good few of these, as the paste dries rather quickly even under the mat. Carefully broaden every second petal slightly, marking a line down the centre. Now do the same for the petals in between. Lift each alternate petal slightly above the one next to it creating the two layers of petals. Bend the wire behind the trumpet at a right angle. Moisten the trumpet with a little glue and stick the petals in place. Add a minute ball of yellow paste behind this and work it down the wire. Now cut an odd scrap of green paste to make the sheath. You need a lot of leaves for the daffodil. Make them using the 'splat' method, crease them slightly and bend them attractively. Dust the trumpet of the daffodil a darker yellow than the petals and add a little beige colouring to the green sheath.

Tulips

Make as many centres for the tulips as you need. These are small balls of paste on 28 gauge wires. Allow them to dry before you make the flowers. Roll out the pink paste fairly finely. Cut out a number of three petalled shapes and cover with a plastic mat. Cup each petal with a ball tool, moisten the small ball with glue and stick the petals around the ball so you cannot see the centre. Repeat this process with another layer of petals ensuring that this time the petals go over the join of the previous layer. Cut long, green oval-shaped pieces of paste, apply glue to the centre, thread the stalk of the tulip through this and pinch it onto the stalk to represent leaves. Dust the flowers and leaves carefully when they are almost dry.

Fill a suitable pot with Staysoft. Start by putting in your daffodil leaves. Add the daffodils and then the tulips. Give the piece a quick spray with matt varnish.

Camellia, Leaves and Twig Arrangement

Requirements

Cold porcelain

36 and 30 gauge wire

120 gauge thread

PME Plunger cutter

Emery board

Colour the paste red, and cut out two shapes using the PME cutter. Soften them on the foam pad. Use 120 gauge thread to make the stamens, hooking it with 30 gauge wire. Bind thread around the outside of the stamens, cutting off the excess. Rub on an emery board to fluff it up. Dust with yellow dust. Pull into the centre of the two overlapped blossom shapes and adjust to look as like a camellia as possible. Use a tiny leaf cutter from one of the manufacturers to make small leaves. These should be on 36 gauge wire. Tape them together with quarter-width tape. Make the twigs as described on page 12 only much smaller.

Find a pot of the right size and shape, Outline the arrangement with the twigs, add the foliage and lastly the flowers which have been lightly varnished.

Fern

Requirements

28 gauge wires

Two smallest cutters from the selection by Fine Cut Cutters

Cut out the leaves on a fine groove on 28 gauge wires. Trim some of the larger leaves so you get a more even variation in height. Frill the edges of the fern leaves gently with a dresden tool and curve the wires. Fill a pot with Staysoft. Dust the leaves and insert them into the Staysoft using a fine nosed pair of pliers or a pair of tweezers. Arrange the leaves attractively and varnish them. Place the pot on a tall stand.

Ornaments

Decorated Goose Egg with Hazelnuts & Leaves

I became interested in egg crafting 10 years ago. An 'egger' (strange word but accepted into the language of the craft), Yvette Smith, came to one of my classes in London to learn how to make sugar flowers. I was very puzzled when she said she didn't decorate cakes, but decorated eggs instead. At the end of the three days she brought in some examples of her work for me to see and I was hooked! I joined the Egg Crafters Guild of Great Britain. Since the advent of cold porcelain this interest has escalated as it is such a good medium to use when decorating eggs.

As far as the purist egger is concerned the egg is all - any decoration must only enhance the egg, not overwhelm it! I prefer the egg to be part of my overall design so often make my cold porcelain pieces larger than would be acceptable in an egg crafting competition.

TP

Materials

Goose egg, blown, sterilised and dry

Wooden or metal egg stand

A card or wrapping paper with a suitable design

Mod Podge

Devcon '5 Minute Epoxy Glue'

Windsor and Newton Acrylic Texturing Paste

Dark brown floristry tape

Liquitex Acrylic Artist colour: Opalescent Green

Equipment

Hollowed-out bath sponge (saturate with water, place in plastic bag, freeze, while frozen cut into egg-shape with a sharp knife. Spin in a washing machine to get rid of excess water. Allow to dry completely)

Kitchen paper

Sharp decoupage scissors

Plum bob on string fastened to the wall hanging completely vertical above a shelf or mantelpiece which is at eye level (you must check with a spirit level that the plum bob is hanging straight and that the shelf is completely level)

Bluetack

Very fine wet and dry sandpaper

Fine make-up sponge

Jar of water

Satay stick and a rubber band

Hairdryer

Old tile

Cocktail sticks

Epoxy glue

Decorating the Egg

1. Choose a fairly large goose egg with a good shape.

2. Very carefully sandpaper the egg to remove any rough patches or dark marks. Wipe carefully with a dry cloth.

3. Use a palette knife to work a small amount of the texturing paste into the blowhole at the top of the egg if there is one. Trim as neatly as possible. Allow to dry.

4. Sand the top of the egg over the texturing paste. If it is not completely smooth repeat this process until it is.

5. While the filler is drying, prepare the card or wrapping paper. If your design is on a thick card split the card and peel away some of the bulk.

6. Paint three even layers of Mod Podge over the picture, allowing it to dry completely between applications. Each layer should be painted on from a different direction. It is best done with your finger. Leave to dry thoroughly.

7. Insert the blunt end of a satay stick into the hole in the base of your egg, push it in very gently (you don't want to accidentally damage the filled hole at the top of the egg). Mark a line on the satay stick with a pencil. Work a piece of Bluetack around the stick at this mark and once again push it into the hole in the egg. The piece of Bluetack should stop the egg from wobbling too much on the end of your stick. Use the elastic band to stop the satay stick from protruding too far into the egg.

8. Moisten the piece of make-up sponge and dip it into the paint you have chosen. Remove most of the paint. Gently dab the paint onto the egg rotating the satay stick so you cover all of the egg. Continue dabbing until all the small bubbles that appear on the surface of the egg are burst. If you have applied too thick a layer of paint this may take a long time. Rinse out your sponge, squeeze it in a piece of kitchen paper and resume the dabbing. It is not essential to get a smooth covering in the first few layers of paint. Blow-dry the paint. Use a medium or low heat - if the heat is too high the paint may bubble more severely.

9. Between layers keep the egg upright on the satay stick by sticking the point into a large piece of styrofoam or something similar. Keep applying thin coats of paint until you have an even coating all over the egg. This may be anything from three coats to five or more. Make sure the last coat of paint is completely dry and then rest the egg, satay stick removed, in the shaped bath sponge.

10. Carefully cut out the picture that has been Mod Podged, removing any background which may spoil the finished design.

11. Float the design in a little hot water (don't panic, it may curl up - you are making your own transfer). When the design becomes cloudy looking very carefully rub off the paper at the back of the design being careful not to remove any of the design itself. If this is the first time you have ever attempted this it may be a good idea to have prepared two designs in case you make a mistake.

12. Very gently lift your transfer from the water, Apply a thin layer of Mod Podge to the egg and position the design where you want it. With a very soft cloth gently press the design onto the egg, being careful not to stretch or distort the design. See there are no air bubbles trapped under the transfer.

13. The length of time and trouble you spend on the next stage will make or break a good découpaged egg. Paint three thin layers of Mod Podge onto the egg letting it dry for eight hours between applications. With the finest wet and dry sandpaper you can buy and a little warm water with a drop of washing up liquid added to it, very gently sandpaper the egg. It should feel smooth to your touch but it will go cloudy. Set aside to dry completely again. Repeat this process as many times as you like. A completely smooth, glass like finish can be achieved with perseverance. For some competition eggs, competitors say they have applied over 100 coats before they have been satisfied, although beginners need not go to those lengths. The egg should feel smooth and you should not be able to feel a raised surface where the design has been applied.

14. Have your chosen stand to hand and your egg ready in its foam nest. Tear up some kitchen paper into minute pieces. Mix a small quantity of Epoxy glue with the same amount of setting agent (this must be accurate or the glue will not set) on an old tile. Keep stirring the mixture. As it becomes cloudy and begins to thicken add some kitchen paper scraps. Work them in.

15. Lift the Epoxy and paper on your cocktail stick and partially fill the hollow in the top of the stand. Do not overfill it, but you need enough paper in the stand so that the base of the egg is not just stuck to the edge of the stand. Push the base of the egg into the stand, carefully removing any excess glue and paper which may ooze out. Quickly position your egg in front of the plum bob at eye level and see that the egg is mounted completely straight on the stand. Turn the stand slowly so you can see it is straight all the way around. Leave alone for a couple of hours until you know the glue is completely set.

16. While you are completing these last stages make the hazelnuts and leaves.

Hazelnuts and Leaves (Corylus avellana)

Materials

Cold Porcelain with Permanent White gouache added

Gouache: Sap Green, Permanent White and Naples Yellow

Craft dust: Sap Green

Sugarcraft dust: Berberis, Nasturtium, Vine and Edelweiss

28 and 26 gauge white wire

20 and 18 gauge wire

Nile Green and Twig floristry tape

Diluted Anita's Satin découpage varnish

Matt spray varnish

Equipment

Great Impressions Hazel Leaf veiner

Orchards Products Six Petal Flower cutters Nos. N4 and N5

Tinkertech Two Christmas Rose cutters (3 sizes)

Nuts

1. Mix a little Naples Yellow gouache into the cold porcelain - it should be a pale ivory in colour. Mix up a little Sap Green paste.

2. Cut two 26 gauge wires into four. Hook one end.

3. Take a marble-sized piece of paste and roll it into a smooth ball. Pinch a sharp point onto the ball and narrow the paste just below this point. Make sure you have nicely shaped 'shoulders'. The hazelnut broadens out to the base. Looked at from the bottom the shape should be oval Moisten a hook on the wire with PVA glue and insert into the centre of the oval base. Fasten onto the wire securely. Use a scriber to mark striations onto the nut and set aside until almost dry. Dust the nut with pale cream dust made from the Berberis and pale beige made by adding a little Nasturtium and Bulrush sugarcraft dust to Edelweiss. When the nuts are completely dry dip them in the varnish diluted with an equal part of water. This should give a faint gleam to the hazelnuts. Dry completely.

Bracts

1. Roll out pale Sap Green cold porcelain fairly thinly. Cut out as many shapes as you need for the nuts, using one or both of the suggested sizes of cutters, depending on the size of the hazelnuts. Cover with a plastic mat until you are ready to use them.

2. Roll a CelStick firmly across one of the shapes increasing the gap between the shapes so you have two lots of three, still joined together. Elongate and broaden all six petal shapes but the two centre petals on either side should be longer than those next to them. Slash the edges of the shapes with a craft knife and then work the edges lightly with a dresden tool. (Remember to work both sides or they will curl.)

3. Moisten the base of a hazelnut with glue and push the wire through the centre of the bract arranging the two lots of bracts along the broad side of the hazelnuts. Pinch the bract firmly against the nut.

4. Repeat this process. Before the bracts dry dust them with Sap Green dust and the tips with a little of the cream and beige dust, with a tiny amount of Nasturtium dust to give a delicate edge.

5. Spray the bracts lightly from underneath with a matt varnish. Try not to get the matt varnish on the nuts.

6. While the bracts are not yet completely set tape them closely together into groups of two or three nuts. They should nestle very tightly together. Set aside to dry.

Leaves

1. Cut 28 and 26 gauge wires into quarters.

2. Roll out pale green paste over a fine groove, moisten a 28 gauge wire with glue, place along the groove allowing the wire to be about two thirds along the finished length of the leaf. Bury the wire with the folded down paste and cut out a leaf using the Christmas Rose cutter with the heavy point as the tip of the leaf.

3. Use a CelStick to gently square up the base of the leaf.

4. Dust the leaf veiner with cornflour and place the ridge into the groove. Press the veiners together.

5. Remove the veined leaf from the veiner and place it on your non-stick board with the wire facing away from you. Starting at the base of the leaf angle the craft knife to cut away small wedges of paste in a flicking movement to give an uneven slightly serrated edge. Repeat the same process on the other side of the leaf, You will soon find out if you can cut the edges in both directions or whether you need to turn the leaf over so you always flick in the same direction.

6. Place the leaf on your Billy's block and very lightly soften the edges of the leaf with your ball tool, being careful not to destroy the veining in the process.

7. Make as many leaves as you need to complete the design, the larger leaves can be made using cream paste.

8. Before they are completely dry dust the leaves; the small leaves with a very little Vine sugarcraft dust and Sap Green craft dust. The larger leaves are dusted with toned down Berberis and Nasturtium at the edges, giving an autumnal tone, and gently over dusted with Sap Green craft dust to blend the colours together. When the leaves are completely dry spray with matt varnish. The backs of the leaves are paler than the front of the leaves. The Great Impressions veiner is quite a sharp veiner and sometimes cuts through the leaves if the paste is not quite thick enough. Don't worry about this as at the time of the year when hazelnuts are ripening the leaves of the bushes have become very tattered. The odd tear adds realism.

Assembly

1. The hazelnuts and leaves are wired into two sprays. One on a 20 gauge wire and the other on an 18 gauge wire. The petioles are taped with quarter-width Nile Green tape, and the stems with half-width Twig tape.

2. Tape the Twig floristry tape over the whole of the stand. Tape the two sprays of hazel together and tape firmly to the stand. Curve into the shapes you require. Dust the floristry tape and seal with PVA glue.

The Head

When undertaking a project of this nature be prepared for thrills and spills. The fact that the paste shrinks has great elements of comedy and tragedy. We find it fun, but you might find it frustrating. The best paste to work with for a project like this or for figure modelling or animal modelling is in our opinion the Asi-es paste. We would not try to do any work of this nature using home-made paste.

Tombi's Tale

The head was done more as an example of what can be done with cold porcelain rather than as a project. The basic form was a polystyrene egg, mounted on the remains of what had been intended as a bonsai tree. The neck was built up first by wrapping twisted soft tissue paper (toilet paper is ideal) around the wire, building it up with the application of a lot of glue. The neck was then built up slowly with many layers of cold porcelain. When undertaking such a venture you must first have an understanding of the musculature of a face and where the main features, eyes, nose and mouth

fit on the basic oval. I was taught that from the top of the head to the chin draw a line halfway down the oval and you have the position for the eyes. A line midway between the eye line and the chin will give you the approximate position for a nose and a line between the nose line and the

chin will give you the position for the mouth. Bisect the oval lengthways and you will find the position of the centre of the nose, the mouth and the area between the eyes.

After marking up the oval the first thing to do is to make a series of balls

in white paste which will become the eyes. Make many in different sizes, but always make two of the same size. Next gouge out holes where the eyes will sit. The next process is to build out the forehead and the back of the head above the nape. You must not add too much paste at a time, you have to be content with a very slow progression. I decided to open the area behind the mouth to give a little more expression to the face and for a week it could have been the model for the picture 'The Scream'. I added paste to the lips on eleven occasions - I made a note of each stage - and I still ended up with a face that needed about a week more work to have been completely finished when we reached the day for the photography. I got fed up with adding pieces of paste to the nose only to find two days later it was once again a cute retousse nose - not what I was aiming for. I then gave it a Jimmy Durante conk and this shrank to the final shape! When modelling faces, figures and animals the shrinkage presents the greatest challenge. I would think on average you need at least 6 weeks patient addition of paste to get the best result.

The jewellery was made using leather punches. The hair was squeezed through a sugar shaper. I decided to make it look like a statue to prevent making a complete hash of it the night before photography. Alan suggested that I paint it gold so that we could go to bed and catch up on some sleep - by now it was four o'clock in the morning! The gold colouring used to cover the piece was Fimo gold powder colour which I added to a little thinned down tacky glue.

Making your own Cold Porcelain

IF YOU SUFFER FROM ASTHMA OR ANY OTHER CHEST COMPLAINT DO NOT ATTEMPT TO MAKE YOUR OWN PASTE, USE MANUFACTURED PASTE.

If you have any doubts at all use a manufactured paste. There is no reason not to as there is now such a variety on the market you should be able to find one which suits you, or you can experiment by mixing the manufactured pastes together until you find a combination which you like.

We started making our own paste because at first there were no pastes on the market which met the criteria we wanted in a cold porcelain paste. After getting the first recipe from Muffie MacKenzie, we both became involved in this new craft and experimented until we found a few recipes which handled well.

It is important to remember health, hygiene and safety. These are extremely important and there are certain precautions that must be taken.

1. Always make the paste in a well-ventilated room. If you have an extractor fan, use it.

2. Wear a mask when making paste.

3. Remember the glues, oils and preservatives used are chemicals and should be treated with respect and caution.

4. If you have any chest problems or are the least bit worried, wear a proper filtering mask when making the paste or use a manufactured paste.

5. Use a separate set of equipment from your cooking utensils for making cold porcelain. Use your intelligence and follow sensible hygiene precautions.

6. Do NOT add aromatherapy oils to the paste to make it smell lovely. An aromatherapist acquaintance has advised against this. She explained these oils are intended to be added to a carrier oil and therefore be diluted. Added to paste which you may be handling you could absorb more oil than is good for you, so it is safer to avoid using them.

You can make a paste from many PVA glues, cornflour, a little oil and a preservative. Experiment if you want to, but do be cautious with what you use. You must ascertain that the products you are using are non-toxic if that is possible.

Four ingredients are used to make cold porcelain: cornflour, glue, preservative and oil.

Glues

The base ingredients for any cold porcelain is PVA glue and cornflour. The particular glue you choose will depend on the type of paste you like using.

a) Elmer's 'Glue-all' makes a soft paste which is fairly white in colour and the container is marked non-toxic.*

b) Impex 'Hi-Tack All Purpose Very Sticky Glue' is another good glue to use as it is almost impossible to break petals made from this glue as they always remain rubbery in texture. Cold porcelain made from this glue is also fairly white. The container is clearly marked non-toxic.†

c) Bison 'Wood Glue' and Bison 'Express Wood Glue' are both good glues to use in making cold porcelain as they make a fairly white paste which is firmer than that made with Elmer's glue or Impex glue. The containers are not marked non-toxic.

d) Liberon 'Super Wood Glue' makes a paste which is tougher to handle and gives the paste a slightly grey tinge. The container is not marked non-toxic. Despite the drawback of the colour of the resulting paste it gives a similar texture to some sugar flower pastes.

Note: Most craft glues are non-toxic, but if the paste is intended for use with children, it is best to make certain that the one you are using is.

*Elmer's glue is a non-toxic American glue which can now be bought from all branches of the Craftworld stores (this does not include the Hobby Craft stores). At the present time they are open in Bristol, Swindon, Milton Keynes and Bolton. They have plans to open a further twelve stores in 1998.

†Impex glue may be obtained from most craft shops, haberdashery shops and floristry wholesalers. Do not confuse this product with Aileen's 'Tacky Glue' which comes in an almost identical container. Although Aileen's glue will make a paste, it does not make a 'flexible' paste.

All glues should be stored at room temperature. They must not be stored in a garage or outhouse as they could become too cold and get damaged.

Preservative

The preservative most commonly used in the making of cold porcelain is sodium benzoate. It is not easily bought from chemist shops as the containers state 'Not for Retail Sale', and most chemists are not prepared to buy a large quantity only to sell you a small amount. Sodium benzoate is used in food production, but in much smaller quantities than we use it. As it is a chemical, use the precautions suggested on the container.

Avoid inhaling sodium benzoate whether in powder form or through the fumes given off during the cooking process.

The wood glues contain anti-fungicides. Paste made from Impex glue can develop a mould even if sodium benzoate is added. By adding a small piece of paste made from a wood glue this mould seems to be eliminated.

Oils

The oils we use in the cold porcelain are baby oil and eucalyptus oil. Some people may not like the smell of eucalyptus oil, in which case, it can be replaced with baby oil. However, a pharmacist acquaintance has said that eucalyptus oil adds an element of elasticity to the paste.

Home-made cold porcelain should be stored at room temperature in sealed plastic bags in a sterile, air-tight container. It must not be refrigerated or frozen.

Tips for Working With Home-made Paste

1. The Impex paste tends to go mouldy if kept for a lengthy period even though it has the preservative in it. If you work a walnut-sized piece of Liberon paste into the Impex paste, kneading in well, the mould does not seem to develop.

2. Knead a small amount of Permanent White gouache into the paste to diminish the translucence and improve the whiteness of the paste.

3. Overcooked paste becomes tough very easily and can start to get unworkable. Learning to cook the paste for the correct length of time is a process of trial and error. It is better to slightly undercook paste and have it a little sticky when you begin to work with it than to have the paste too tough to start with. If you do overcook a batch, break off small pieces of the paste and knead softer paste into it. While working with paste if it toughens up, try adding a few drops of warm water into the paste and kneading well.

SENSIBLE PRECAUTIONS

1. Wear a mask when making paste.

2. Check labels to see if material is toxic.

3. Read instructions and warnings on material containers.

4. Keep materials out of the reach of children and animals.

5. Supervise children at all times.

6. Do not use aromatherapy oils.

7. Do not INHALE sodium benzoate.

8. Exercise care when using warm or hot materials.

WARNING

The 'recipes' are tried and tested and we are not aware of any adverse reactions from anybody making them or using products made from the pastes. You should however take reasonable care, especially if you know e.g. that you suffer from any allergy or other susceptability. If in any doubt seek medical advice.

Tombi's Paste

I like using a fairly strong, flexible paste for most petals and leaves. I find this paste provides the qualities in cold porcelain that I am looking for. For small delicate flowers I use flexible (bendy/Impex) paste and very often I mix this paste with some of mine to get the consistency I require for the type of flower I am making.

Ingredients

40ml (2 tablespoons and 1 dessertspoon) baby oil

5ml (1 teaspoon) eucalyptus oil

2.5ml ($^1/_2$ teaspoon) sodium benzoate

125ml ($^1/_2$ cup) Liberon 'Super Wood Glue'

125ml ($^1/_2$ cup) Bison 'Extra Wood Glue'

170g (1 cup) cornflour

Equipment

Non-stick pan

Measuring spoons and measures

Wooden spoon

Spatula

Non-stick board

Cling film

Sealable plastic bags

Air-tight container

1. Measure the oils into the non-stick saucepan. Carefully add the sodium benzoate and the glues. Stir these ingredients together until they are like a thick cream. Add the cornflour and stir to a thick paste. Put over a medium heat and stirring continuously, cook until the saucepan is completely clean. From time to time remove from the heat, scrape the un-cooked paste from the spoon and then continue cooking. This paste will appear to go very lumpy during the cooking process but this is quite normal.

2. Turn the paste onto a non-stick board and knead firmly (as for bread) until the paste is smooth and whiter than it was before kneading. If it sticks to your hands while kneading just continue to knead. Do not add extra cornflour or stop to wash your hands. Wrap in cling film and allow to cool. Once cold knead the paste again, putting it into a fresh piece of cling film and place in a plastic bag, then into the sterilised, air-tight container.

Alan's Paste

(also known as 'Flexible (Bendy) Paste')

This paste is wonderful for making delicate flowers and leaves such as jasmine and birds-foot ivy as the paste bends rather than breaking. It isn't the easiest of pastes to work with as it is a soft paste which has a tendency to stick to cutters. Brushing the cutters with a little cold cream prevents this to a large extent. (Always keep a new, clean toothbrush to hand to brush paste off your cutters.) Less oil is used in this recipe than in the previous one as craft glues cannot absorb as much oil as the wood glues.

This paste can be mixed with various proportions of a paste that dries hard giving a finished paste that has easier modelling qualities yet still retains a high degree of flexibility.

Ingredients

30ml (2 tablespoons) baby oil

2.5ml ($^1/_2$ teaspoon) sodium benzoate

250ml (1 cup) Impex 'Hi-tack All Purpose Very Sticky Glue'

170g (1 cup) cornflour

A walnut-sized piece of cold porcelain made with PVA glue

Equipment

Non-stick pan

Measuring spoons

Measuring cups

Wooden spoon

Spatula

Non-stick board

Cling film

Sealable plastic bags

Air-tight container

1. Mix these ingredients together (in the order given above) in a non-stick saucepan and cook over a moderate heat until the paste gathers around and then leaves the spoon. (The craft glues require less cooking time than that needed for the wood glues.) Turn onto a non-stick board and knead until smooth and white.

2. If the paste sticks to you do not add extra cornflour, just continue to knead the paste until your hands are clean. If the paste sticks to the non-stick board this generally indicates that it has not been cooked for long enough and should be returned to the saucepan for a slightly longer cooking period.

3. Wrap in cling film. When the paste is cold knead it again and wrap it in a fresh piece of cling film before placing into a sealed plastic bag in a sterile, air-tight container.

Equipment

The following items are all things that the dedicated cold porcelain user will require. We have assumed this as a standard kit, and therefore the equipment lists for each project only contain things which are specific to that piece, such as a particular cutter.

Most of these items can be bought from good sugarcraft shops and art and craft shops.

Non-stick board

Non-stick grooved board

Non-stick rolling pin

CelSticks of various sizes

Billy's block or CelPad (foam pad)

Cold porcelain metal ball tools and veiners (you can use plastic ball tools although cold porcelain tends to stick to the plastic tools more easily than to the metal tools)

Dresden tool

Realistic leaf and petal veiners

Cutters (both plastic and metal)

Holly Products Ceramic Silk Veining Tool

Frilling sticks of various thicknesses

Blunted cocktail sticks

Sharp scissors (straight and curved)

Wire cutters

Fine-nosed electricians pliers

Tweezers (curved, angled and straight)

Porcupine quill

Plastic mat

PVA glue and monojet glue dispenser

Watered-down glue in a small, lidded pot

Craft knives and scalpels

Hairdryer

Cornflour bag

Pot of cornflour

Pot of water

Designer gouache paints

Oil paints

Oil thinners

Craft dusts

Colour fast sugarcraft dusting colours

Squires Kitchen Alabaster Bridal Satin dust

Barrier hand cream

Cold cream

Clean unused toothbrush (for cleaning cutters)

Mixture of brushes (for oil paints, for dusting and for painting fine lines)

Needle tool

Scribing tool

Dimpled foam

Tape shredder

Dedication

We would like to dedicate this book to our very dear friend Peggy Green

Acknowledgements

We would like to acknowledge the information shared with us by Muffie MacKenzie, Cynthia Venn, Regina from Brazil and Titi Pena from Argentina.

Suppliers

CELCRAFTS
Springfield House
Gate Helmsley
York
YO4 1NF
Tel: 01759 371447
Ready-made cold porcelain, craft dusts and tools.
Mail Order

COUNTRY CUTTERS
Lower Trefaldu
Dingestow
Monmouth
Gwent
NP5 4BQ
Tel: 01600 740448
Wide range of cutters - produce a number of unusual ones.
Mail Order

GREAT IMPRESSIONS
Greenlea
14 Studley Drive
Swarland
Morpeth
Northumberland
NE65 9JT
Tel: 01670 787061
Veiners (a speciality), moulds and transfers.
Mail Order

HOLLY PRODUCTS
Holly Cottage
Hassall Green
Sandbach
CW11 4YA
Tel: 01270 761403
Moulds, embossers, patterns and tools.
Mail Order

JEM CUTTERS
PO Box 115
Kloof 3640
Republic of South Africa
Tel: 0027 31 701 1431
Vast range of cutters - available from most UK retail outlets.
UK distributors: Guy Paul and Co. Ltd. Tel: 01480 472545 and Cake Art Ltd. Tel: 01823 321532

ORCHARD PRODUCTS
51 Hallyburton Road
Hove
East Sussex
BN3 7GP
Tel: 01273 419418
Manufacturers and suppliers of fine quality sugarcraft cutters, tools and cold porcelain.
Shop and Mail Order

PAT-A-CAKE
584 King Standing Road
Birmingham
B44 9SH
Tel: 0121 3848446
Variety of sugarcraft tools particularly miniature cutters.
Shop and Mail Order

THE SCIENTIFIC WIRE COMPANY
18 Raven Road
London
E18 1HW
Tel: 0181 505 0002
Suppliers of 36 gauge silk-covered wire.
Mail Order

SQUIRES KITCHEN SUGARCRAFT
Squires House
3 Waverley Lane
Farnham
Surrey
GU9 8BB
Tel: 01252 711749
Sugarcraft dusts, tools and equipment. Ready-made cold porcelain paste. Craft colours - Marble Art range.
Shop, School, Mail Order

SUGAR CELEBRATIONS
176A Manchester Road
Swindon
SN1 1TU
Tel: 01793 513549
A wide range of cake decorating equipment and accessories.
Shop and Mail Order

TINKERTECH TWO
40 Langdon Road
Parkstone
Poole
Dorset
BH14 9EH
Tel: 01202 738049
A wide range of metal cutters, particularly flowers and leaves. Widely available from sugarcraft shops.

PUBLICATIONS

MEREHURST
Ferry House
51 - 57 Lacy Road
Putney
London
SW15 1PR
Tel: 0181 3551480
Publisher of many cake decorating and sugarcraft titles.

SUGARCRAFT MAGAZINE
Alfred House
Hones Business Park
Farnham
Surrey
GU9 8BB
Tel: 01252 727572
Monthly cake decorating and sugarcraft magazine offering new ideas and inspirations to the sugarcrafter and cold porcelain artist.

SOCIETIES

PORCELAINA SOCIETY
Mrs Pat Cairns *(Secretary)*
46 Meadow Way
Tottington
Bury
Lancashire
B18 3HU

Index